Complete Horoscope

Monthly astrological forecasts for 2024

TATIANA BORSCH

Translated from Russian by Sonja Swenson

AstraArt Books is an imprint of Coinflow limited, Cyprus
Published by Coinflow Limited, Cyprus
For queries please contact: tatianaborsch@yahoo.com

ISBN 978-9925-609-44-4 (paperback)
ISBN 978-9925-609-45-1 (ebook)

Contents

General Astrological Forecast for 2024

We are embarking on yet another difficult year, which can generally be divided into two very different periods. During the first half of the year, Jupiter, which is the most powerful planet in our solar system, will be in the sign of Taurus, creating a favorable aspect with Saturn. That means that both peoples' lives and events on the political stage will play out rather predictably.

This is a very good time for China – it will continue to expand its power, both economically and politically, which will of course impact its position in the global arena. We might see successful negotiations regarding Taiwan.

The first half of 2024 will also be very positive for India. Its economy is surging – over the next three to four years, it will be able to make significant investments in resolving problems such as poverty and develop its infrastructure and industry. It will become a global economic leader.

However, things are not so rosy in the Old World – Europe, where economic drivers such as Germany, are going through a troublesome astrological period. In India, this is known as Sade Sati (Saturn's transit through the sign of the Moon, which often includes the Moon's neighboring zodiac sign). Usually, this period lasts about three years. Each country will experience things its own way. For Germany, this most likely means an economic slowdown and domestic political and social turbulence. This is a trend that began in 2022 and will last for about three years.

Obviously we won't see any repeats of Brexit in 2024, though this may appear somewhat later. Over the next three to four years, the EU will undergo serious changes, and the European Commission might lose some of its powers, as dictating the rules of the game to the world will become much more difficult.

With regard to the United States, 2024 might be particularly difficult. Pluto is returning to its position in the US birth chart, and this is very important, as it will be in the sector of the sky responsible for the banking system, finances, and even society's emotional state.

Pluto is the planet responsible for purification and renewal, but it also brings the destruction of anything obsolete, which may trigger global crises, which are inevitable with any change in the system. That is why in 2024, economic strife may trigger demonstrations against the current government, as well as a serious struggle for power among members of the ruling class.

During the second half of the year, the United States may lose a lot of allies – this trend will continue into 2025. Perhaps this will be due to a stronger China, Russia, and India, or alternatively, growing economic problems. The US will weaken in its role as the hegemon.

The US presidential elections in 2024 may bring a repeat of what we saw in 2020. It is hard to imagine Joe Biden hanging onto the presidency. He will leave. But these elections will be full of scandal, most likely due to Trump's bombastic speeches.

During the second half of the year, Jupiter will be in Gemini, which supports Trump, as he himself is a Gemini. During the first half of the year, however, despite his histrionics, Trump will spend the first half of 2024 busy with legal troubles that began in 2023. But during the second half of the year, he will be at the center of society's attention – what more could a politician need? Both Trump and Ron de Santis have a good shot at the presidency. De Santis's birth time is unknown, but I think he has a good chance.

Another thorn in the US's side may be the situation in the Middle East, which is already unstable, but in 2024, some kind of military confrontation may break out.

Jupiter in Gemini creates a negative aspect with Saturn, which will close in mid-August, and which portends difficulties for the global economy. This means a situation that is highly unstable, with volatile markets and trouble in the banking sector.

We might, however, see scientific breakthroughs – perhaps new technology and discoveries await in the hands of the world's young and talented scientists.

Fashion will become more feminine and elegant during the first half of the year. Jupiter in Taurus means that we can expect more fitted silhouettes, and perhaps greater focus on traditional garb. Beige will be the color of the day, as will all hues of gold and brown. As always, black will be in demand. Clothing will be monochromatic.

During the second half of the year, we can expect light and dark blue, green, and unusual color combinations. The look will be unkempt and carefree, with a greater focus on youth fashions than the classics. Jupiter in Gemini also suggests flowing, translucent fabrics.

All year long, the weather will be unstable, with flooding affecting coastal countries and islands. We might see a more serious version of what has already happened in several regions of the world. During the second half of the year, many countries can expect to deal with strong winds and tornadoes.

While we can say that everyone has their own fate, global circumstances often are indirectly reflected in each of our lives.

Despite all the ups and downs, the first half of 2024 is the best time for getting married, having babies, or buying real estate.

During the second half of the year, I would not recommend any long-distance travel, starting any legal proceedings, or making important decisions about moving. During this time, many relationships will fall apart, if things were already on the rocks. But you can find out more about that in my forecast for each Zodiac sign.

Best of luck in 2024!

Astrologist Tatiana Borsch

2024 Overview for Virgo

2024 is a chance for you to leave the past behind and start life with a clean slate. You will have an extraordinary chance to reach the top of what you want, but you will have to put up a serious fight in order to make it happen.

Work

The favorable changes that began during the second half of 2023 will continue in 2024. Many Virgos will link their interests to business partners in other cities or abroad and cooperate to benefit both parties. Alternatively, you might move or open a business in another city or abroad.

2024 is a wonderful time for studies, as well as undertaking serious work on yourself, especially during the first half of the year.

Employees might see a 180-degree turn in their professional development – perhaps a job offer far from home, a move, or frequent travel.

During the first half of the year, from January to June, you will see anything work-related play out smoothly, without a hitch or any trouble.

During the second half of the year, however, things will become more difficult. Starting in August, business owners will have a serious disagreement with their partners. They may have clashing views over the direction their business should take, or perhaps over various

January

New York Time				London Time		
Calendar Day	Lunar Day	Lunar Day Start Time		Calendar Day	Lunar Day	Lunar Day Start Time
01/01/24	21	10.18 PM		01/01/24	21	10.02 PM
02/01/24	22	11.16 PM		02/01/24	22	11.08 PM
04/01/24	23	12.14 AM		04/01/24	23	12.14 AM
05/01/24	24	1.14 AM		05/01/24	24	1.22 AM
06/01/24	25	2.16 AM		06/01/24	25	2.32 AM
07/01/24	26	3.20 AM		07/01/24	26	3.44 AM
08/01/24	27	4.26 AM		08/01/24	27	4.57 AM
09/01/24	28	5.30 AM		09/01/24	28	6.07 AM
10/01/24	29	6.31 AM		10/01/24	29	7.10 AM
11/01/24	1	6.58 AM		11/01/24	30	8.03 AM
11/01/24	2	7.26 AM		11/01/24	1	11.58 AM
12/01/24	3	8.13 AM		12/01/24	2	8.44 AM
13/01/24	4	8.53 AM		13/01/24	3	9.16 AM
14/01/24	5	9.27 AM		14/01/24	4	9.42 AM
15/01/24	6	9.59 AM		15/01/24	5	10.05 AM
16/01/24	7	10.29 AM		16/01/24	6	10.25 AM
17/01/24	8	10.58 AM		17/01/24	7	10.45 AM
18/01/24	9	11.29 AM		18/01/24	8	11.07 AM
19/01/24	10	12.04 PM		19/01/24	9	11.32 AM
20/01/24	11	12.42 PM		20/01/24	10	12.02 PM
21/01/24	12	1.26 PM		21/01/24	11	12.39 PM
22/01/24	13	2.16 PM		22/01/24	12	1.25 PM
23/01/24	14	3.11 PM		23/01/24	13	2.19 PM
24/01/24	15	4.10 PM		24/01/24	14	3.21 PM
25/01/24	16	5.10 PM		25/01/24	15	4.27 PM
26/01/24	17	6.10 PM		26/01/24	16	5.35 PM
27/01/24	18	7.10 PM		27/01/24	17	6.43 PM
28/01/24	19	8.08 PM		28/01/24	18	7.50 PM
29/01/24	20	9.06 PM		29/01/24	19	8.56 PM
30/01/24	21	10.04 PM		30/01/24	20	10.01 PM
31/01/24	22	11.02 PM		31/01/24	21	11.08 PM

You can find the description of each lunar day in the chapter "A Guide to The Moon Cycle and Lunar Days"

January is a time to focus on your family and private life. Spend it being a bit of a shut-in and forget about work for a while. Your work will still be there tomorrow, after all.

Work

During the first 20 days of the month, don't expect to see a lot of success at work. The exception is those working in the creative professions – actors, artists, singers, musicians, and anyone who works in the arts. These Virgos will be on the receiving end of accolades from the public, handsome royalties, and other gifts from capricious Fortune. If you work in another field, expect to have a lot of free time until January 20, before putting your nose to the grindstone as the month draws to a close.

For many Virgos, there are changes underway at work – what once looked stable, promising, and financially sound has proven otherwise. This is not a new development, but something that has been brewing for a few years now, and the time has come to turn the page and start over with a clean slate. Expect new plans and a complete overhaul of your path in life this month. That may be related to a move, or perhaps a new business or job. You have a full plate, plans to make, and in general, plenty to live for.

Your ties with colleagues in other cities or abroad are coming along nicely, and you may take a trip, successfully resolve some legal issues, or those related to residence abroad.

The good news is that in January, you will renew some old connections, and that may happen while you are traveling or with people from somewhere faraway.

Money

Financially speaking, you might describe January as uncertain. Your income is low, but your expenses are, too. You can expect Fortune to shine down on you, for example, nothing is stopping you from buying a lottery ticket. Your chances of winning are high.

Love and family

January is a time to immerse yourself in your personal life. During the first few days of the month, married couples can expect some friction on various issues, but things will improve drastically after the 15th.

Those who are divorced or in a marriage on the rocks will end up coming together over concerns over your children, and you might even take a family trip together. If you want to soften your spouse's heart, now is the time.

Unmarried couples will also have a good second half of January. Your relationship will grow warmer, and you might travel together, which will be an opportunity to both enjoy yourselves and iron out any contradictions.

Those who are single might have an interesting encounter and exciting romance. Even if it doesn't lead to marriage, it will certainly brighten your month.

Health

You are feeling energetic this month and have no reason to fear falling ill. The best time to change up your image, go shopping, or undergo any aesthetic surgery would be after January 10.

February

New York Time		
Calendar Day	Lunar Day	Lunar Day Start Time
02/02/24	23	12.02 AM
03/02/24	24	1.04 AM
04/02/24	25	2.07 AM
05/02/24	26	3.11 AM
06/02/24	27	4.12 AM
07/02/24	28	5.10 AM
08/02/24	29	6.00 AM
09/02/24	30	6.44 AM
09/02/24	1	6.00 PM
10/02/24	2	7.22 AM
11/02/24	3	7.56 AM
12/02/24	4	8.28 AM
13/02/24	5	8.59 AM
14/02/24	6	9.30 AM
15/02/24	7	10.04 AM
16/02/24	8	10.42 AM
17/02/24	9	11.25 AM
18/02/24	10	12.13 PM
19/02/24	11	1.06 PM
20/02/24	12	2.03 PM
21/02/24	13	3.03 PM
22/02/24	14	4.03 PM
23/02/24	15	5.02 PM
24/02/24	16	6.01 PM
25/02/24	17	6.59 PM
26/02/24	18	7.57 PM
27/02/24	19	8.55 PM
28/02/24	20	9.54 PM
29/02/24	21	10.54 PM

London Time		
Calendar Day	Lunar Day	Lunar Day Start Time
02/02/24	22	12.16 AM
03/02/24	23	1.25 AM
04/02/24	24	2.36 AM
05/02/24	25	3.46 AM
06/02/24	26	4.51 AM
07/02/24	27	5.48 AM
08/02/24	28	6.35 AM
09/02/24	29	7.12 AM
09/02/24	1	11.00 PM
10/02/24	2	7.41 AM
11/02/24	3	8.06 AM
12/02/24	4	8.28 AM
13/02/24	5	8.49 AM
14/02/24	6	9.11 AM
15/02/24	7	9.36 AM
16/02/24	8	10.05 AM
17/02/24	9	10.39 AM
18/02/24	10	11.22 AM
19/02/24	11	12.14 PM
20/02/24	12	1.13 PM
21/02/24	13	2.18 PM
22/02/24	14	3.25 PM
23/02/24	15	4.32 PM
24/02/24	16	5.39 PM
25/02/24	17	6.45 PM
26/02/24	18	7.51 PM
27/02/24	19	8.57 PM
28/02/24	20	10.04 PM
29/02/24	21	11.13 PM

You can find the description of each lunar day in the chapter "A Guide to The Moon Cycle and Lunar Days"

This month, many Virgos will run into obstacles, and might be feeling less than confident. Rely on your mind and sound logic – in this case, the stars will provide an answer to many of your problems.

Work

For most of the month, you will be running on fumes as you run around dealing with difficult tasks at work, but at the last minute, all of your efforts might go to waste.

Both business owners and managers will deal with disagreements with their colleagues from other cities or abroad, who might suddenly impose conditions that are far from what you had earlier agreed on.

You might also face inspections or have old legal problems unexpectedly come back into your life.

In the face of any difficulties, you can count on support from previous business partners, or perhaps someone close to you. They might act as an intermediary or provide moral and material support.

Through your joint efforts, some of these issues will be resolved by March, and the others will disappear somewhat later.

Students might face challenges in February, especially if their studies have something to do with another country.

February is also a good time to both renew old ties and make new connections.

Money

Financially speaking, February is looking somewhat bumpy. While you won't find yourself penniless, you are spending a lot of money. That may be due to business or perhaps your personal life.

Love and family

Your personal life is more stable than things at work. Those who recently endured a breakup will be pleased to discover that any cracks in the relationship can be mended with a little hard work. In many cases, your children will be of assistance, as taking care of them builds a bridge between former spouses.

Though the situation is not ideal, there is still a chance of reconciliation or at least healthy communication, but it will require restraint, humility, understanding, and forgiveness.

Couples who get along will be pleased to see that their children are on a successful streak.

Be especially careful traveling in February, including with your documents and laws in foreign countries.

Health

Those who manage to find harmony at home and at work are likely to run into health issues this month, especially if they are elderly or weakened and therefore especially vulnerable to pressure from the heavens. If that is you, be sure to take protective measures when it comes to any chronic illnesses and take care of yourself.

Those who are young and healthy would be wise to be careful when traveling or behind the wheel. All month long, the likelihood of traffic accidents is very high, with the worst between February 17 and 27.

March

New York Time			London Time		
Calendar Day	Lunar Day	Lunar Day Start Time	Calendar Day	Lunar Day	Lunar Day Start Time
01/03/24	22	11.56 PM	02/03/24	22	12.22 AM
03/03/24	23	12.57 AM	03/03/24	23	1.30 AM
04/03/24	24	1.58 AM	04/03/24	24	2.36 AM
05/03/24	25	2.55 AM	05/03/24	25	3.35 AM
06/03/24	26	3.48 AM	06/03/24	26	4.25 AM
07/03/24	27	4.34 AM	07/03/24	27	5.05 AM
08/03/24	28	5.14 AM	08/03/24	28	5.38 AM
09/03/24	29	5.50 AM	09/03/24	29	6.05 AM
10/03/24	1	4.02 AM	10/03/24	30	6.28 AM
10/03/24	2	6.23 AM	10/03/24	1	9.02 AM
11/03/24	3	6.55 AM	11/03/24	2	6.50 AM
12/03/24	4	7.27 AM	12/03/24	3	7.12 AM
13/03/24	5	8.01 AM	13/03/24	4	7.36 AM
14/03/24	6	8.38 AM	14/03/24	5	8.04 AM
15/03/24	7	9.21 AM	15/03/24	6	8.37 AM
16/03/24	8	10.08 AM	16/03/24	7	9.19 AM
17/03/24	9	11.01 AM	17/03/24	8	10.08 AM
18/03/24	10	11.57 AM	18/03/24	9	11.06 AM
19/03/24	11	12.56 PM	19/03/24	10	12.09 PM
20/03/24	12	1.56 PM	20/03/24	11	1.16 PM
21/03/24	13	2.55 PM	21/03/24	12	2.23 PM
22/03/24	14	3.54 PM	22/03/24	13	3.30 PM
23/03/24	15	4.52 PM	23/03/24	14	4.36 PM
24/03/24	16	5.50 PM	24/03/24	15	5.42 PM
25/03/24	17	6.48 PM	25/03/24	16	6.48 PM
26/03/24	18	7.47 PM	26/03/24	17	7.55 PM
27/03/24	19	8.47 PM	27/03/24	18	9.03 PM
28/03/24	20	9.48 PM	28/03/24	19	10.12 PM
29/03/24	21	10.50 PM	29/03/24	20	11.21 PM
30/03/24	22	11.50 PM	31/03/24	21	12.27 AM

You can find the description of each lunar day in the chapter "A Guide to The Moon Cycle and Lunar Days"

In March, you will become a part of a complex game, which may consume your entire surroundings. That goes for both work and your love life.

Work

For many Virgos, your professional interests still lie with developing your relationship with colleagues in other cities or abroad.

During the first 10 days of the month, you might go on a travel or meet with colleagues and strengthen old ties or make new ones. However, despite the friendly atmosphere, not everything will run so smoothly. During the New Moon, from March 9 to 11, you might again hit obstacles, which might look different. They may involve dealing with laws in other countries, or possibly handling legal matters.

It's not worth trying to go it alone. An old business partner might serve as an intermediary and you can expect to grow much closer in March.

Business owners and managers would be wise to keep an eye on their subordinates. Their zeal might help, but it might also hurt. Employees should be careful with the way they communicate with colleagues and avoid any intrigue. It's just not worth it.

Money

Financially, March is a neutral time for you. Your income is moderate, but your expenses are modest, too. In difficult cases, you might lean on a business partner, spouse, or loved one for help.

Love and family

As usual, nothing is quiet in your personal life, either. For a year now, Saturn, a harsh and unforgiving planet, has been in the sector of the sky responsible for marriage and long-term connections. This is why so many people have been reconsidering their relationships, and in some

The New Moon and eclipse on April 8 will force you to stop, take a look around, and batten down the hatches.

Work

In addition to the harsh influence of the eclipse, your ruler, Mercury, will be in retrograde from April 2-25, meaning that any Virgos who are part of the working world can expect to face a series of challenges. During this time, it is not worth getting into any major business, starting new projects, or trying to make too much progress. It is, however, a great time to cross your t's and dot your i's or address any cumbersome administrative issues.

Your relationship with business partners from afar is moving along with varying success. You might have difficult negotiations over financial and material issues. You will not resolve this quickly, but by May, things will be looking rosier on both sides.

If you are planning on travel or on opening a business in another city or abroad, this month may bring a variety of administrative troubles and you will have to overcome them on your own.

April is a tough time for most employees. Your colleagues and managers will notice both your qualities and your shortcomings, so be very attentive and don't lose sight of the details.

Carefully plan any business trips in April, and if you can, put them off until May.

Money

April is also a hard time for your wallet. You have few expenses, but they are probably related to either business or your personal problems.

You can expect tense negotiations with business partners over financial assistance or investments. Many will be thinking about taking out credit and filling out forms with this aim.

Love and family

Those who are more focused on their personal lives might have to grapple with challenging household issues. Those who are moving somewhere far away will be busy dealing with their home, or perhaps buying a new residence or making repairs right where they are.

Divorcing or separated couples might decide how to divide up their finances, and you can expect a real breakthrough here. Many couples may be seriously wondering if their relationship is really over for good, or if there is some way to reconcile. Here, the ball is in your partner's court, and all you can do is listen to your own intuition. Right now, it speaks the truth.

A major trend this month will be renewing your ties to old friends, acquaintances, or a former flame. Anyone new you meet between April 2 and 25 is probably not as reliable or trustworthy as he or she appears at first glance.

Health

All month long, you might feel a bit under the weather. Avoid any physical stress right now and be sure to relax instead.

Those who are weakened, or elderly should be especially attentive and take preventive measures ahead of time.

You might see a resurfacing of old illnesses or accidents this month. The likelihood is very high.

May

New York Time			London Time		
Calendar Day	Lunar Day	Lunar Day Start Time	Calendar Day	Lunar Day	Lunar Day Start Time
01/05/24	23	2.07 AM	01/05/24	23	2.38 AM
02/05/24	24	2.43 AM	02/05/24	24	3.07 AM
03/05/24	25	3.16 AM	03/05/24	25	3.31 AM
04/05/24	26	3.47 AM	04/05/24	26	3.53 AM
05/05/24	27	4.18 AM	05/05/24	27	4.14 AM
06/05/24	28	4.49 AM	06/05/24	28	4.35 AM
07/05/24	29	5.23 AM	07/05/24	29	4.59 AM
07/05/24	1	11.24 PM	08/05/24	1	4.24 AM
08/05/24	2	6.02 AM	08/05/24	2	5.27 AM
09/05/24	3	6.46 AM	09/05/24	3	6.02 AM
10/05/24	4	7.36 AM	10/05/24	4	6.46 AM
11/05/24	5	8.33 AM	11/05/24	5	7.39 AM
12/05/24	6	9.33 AM	12/05/24	6	8.41 AM
13/05/24	7	10.34 AM	13/05/24	7	9.48 AM
14/05/24	8	11.36 AM	14/05/24	8	10.57 AM
15/05/24	9	12.36 PM	15/05/24	9	12.06 PM
16/05/24	10	1.35 PM	16/05/24	10	1.13 PM
17/05/24	11	2.33 PM	17/05/24	11	2.19 PM
18/05/24	12	3.31 PM	18/05/24	12	3.25 PM
19/05/24	13	4.29 PM	19/05/24	13	4.32 PM
20/05/24	14	5.29 PM	20/05/24	14	5.39 PM
21/05/24	15	6.31 PM	21/05/24	15	6.49 PM
22/05/24	16	7.33 PM	22/05/24	16	7.59 PM
23/05/24	17	8.36 PM	23/05/24	17	9.09 PM
24/05/24	18	9.37 PM	24/05/24	18	10.15 PM
25/05/24	19	10.33 PM	25/05/24	19	11.13 PM
26/05/24	20	11.24 PM	27/05/24	20	12.02 AM
28/05/24	21	12.07 AM	28/05/24	21	12.40 AM
29/05/24	22	12.45 AM	29/05/24	22	1.11 AM
30/05/24	23	1.19 AM	30/05/24	23	1.36 AM
31/05/24	24	1.50 AM	31/05/24	24	1.58 AM

You can find the description of each lunar day in the chapter "A Guide to The Moon Cycle and Lunar Days"

The time for ideas and long-term planning has concluded, and now, it's time for you to roll up your sleeves and get to work!

Work

You have embarked on a very important phase at work. Those who lost ground in the past are gradually recovering, and here, you can get back in the saddle.

Those who are planning a move or to open a business in another city or abroad seem to have achieved what they wanted. Ahead, expect a lot of work, a new professional cycle, which will bring you utmost success for the next three to four years.

In one way or another, all Virgos will be impacted by these new trends. You will be able to start a new business or job if you stay right where you are, as well, or perhaps you will go back to school for something new. The stars support and value all of these steps.

Initially, you will be able to count on old friends and former business partners. But it is worth remembering that that is only temporary. Later on, things will change, and not necessarily for the better. For various reasons, by the fall or winter of 2024, your relationship will have soured with people who might be lending a helping hand right now, and you will have to part ways. Remember and act accordingly.

Money

Your finances are improving, slowly but surely. This is especially noticeable during the last 10 days of May and in June.

Expect to receive the largest sums on May 9, 10, 18-20, and 28-30.

Love and family

Your personal life looks less tranquil. Harsh Saturn is firmly entrenched in the sector of the sky responsible for marriage and all long-term relationships, and that does not bode well for most Virgos.

For now, you can still count on support from your better half, even if you have recently fought.

Divorcing spouses might have to communicate for various reasons, and that will be surprisingly peaceful. In some cases, that will be very beneficial to both parties. You may have your children or a shared business to thank for that, or perhaps there are simply some burning embers of feelings left.

If that is the case, you might try to start over with a clean slate.

But remember, that later on, this situation will unexpectedly repeat itself, and things will not turn out quite the way you had hoped.

In addition to encounters with an old flame, the stars promise new acquaintances, who might develop into a passionate romance. You have plenty of choices right now, and that's a good thing.

Health

In May, you are healthy, energetic, a social butterfly, attractive, and making lasting impressions with everyone Fate throws your way.

June

New York Time		
Calendar Day	Lunar Day	Lunar Day Start Time
01/06/24	25	2.19 AM
02/06/24	26	2.49 AM
03/06/24	27	3.21 AM
04/06/24	28	3.56 AM
05/06/24	29	4.37 AM
06/06/24	30	5.24 AM
06/06/24	1	8.40 AM
07/06/24	2	6.18 AM
08/06/24	3	7.17 AM
09/06/24	4	8.19 AM
10/06/24	5	9.22 AM
11/06/24	6	10.23 AM
12/06/24	7	11.23 AM
13/06/24	8	12.22 PM
14/06/24	9	1.20 PM
15/06/24	10	2.18 PM
16/06/24	11	3.17 PM
17/06/24	12	4.17 PM
18/06/24	13	5.19 PM
19/06/24	14	6.22 PM
20/06/24	15	7.25 PM
21/06/24	16	8.24 PM
22/06/24	17	9.18 PM
23/06/24	18	10.06 PM
24/06/24	19	10.46 PM
25/06/24	20	11.22 PM
26/06/24	21	11.53 PM
28/06/24	22	12.23 AM
29/06/24	23	12.52 AM
30/06/24	24	1.23 AM

London Time		
Calendar Day	Lunar Day	Lunar Day Start Time
01/06/24	25	2.19 AM
02/06/24	26	2.39 AM
03/06/24	27	3.01 AM
04/06/24	28	3.26 AM
05/06/24	29	3.57 AM
06/06/24	30	4.36 AM
06/06/24	1	1.40 PM
07/06/24	2	5.25 AM
08/06/24	3	6.24 AM
09/06/24	4	7.30 AM
10/06/24	5	8.39 AM
11/06/24	6	9.49 AM
12/06/24	7	10.58 AM
13/06/24	8	12.05 PM
14/06/24	9	1.11 PM
15/06/24	10	2.17 PM
16/06/24	11	3.21 PM
17/06/24	12	4.32 PM
18/06/24	13	5.42 PM
19/06/24	14	6.53 PM
20/06/24	15	8.01 PM
21/06/24	16	9.04 PM
22/06/24	17	9.57 PM
23/06/24	18	10.40 PM
24/06/24	19	11.14 PM
25/06/24	20	11.42 PM
27/06/24	21	12.05 AM
28/06/24	22	12.25 AM
29/06/24	23	12.45 AM
30/06/24	24	1.06 AM

You can find the description of each lunar day in the chapter "A Guide to The Moon Cycle and Lunar Days"

For you, June is one of the busiest times of the year. You have made the right choice, and there is a long road ahead, but you're only just beginning.

Work

The best time for anything work-related is the first 10 days of June. During this time, you will come up with brilliant ideas, and a real chance to bring them to life, too.

For many business owners and managers of every level, your priorities are still your relationship with colleagues in other cities or abroad. You can expect some impressive professional achievements here, which will breathe new life into your business.

Not everything will turn out as you might have hoped, and this will become clear during the second 10 days of the month. During this time, you might run into serious disagreements with business partners over your business development, or perhaps financial issues.

Some of these problems will involve colleagues from far away. Things will improve during the last 10 days of June, when an old friend or someone highly placed in society might bring a peace offering. Thanks to them, your opponents will simmer down, or at least be open to a compromise.

Employees might receive a new job with great opportunities for the future, and you might even start this month.

Money

Financially, this is not a bad time for you at all. You will have money coming in regularly, and significantly more than usual. Most of your expenses will take place during the last part of the month, and they might even be pleasant.

Love and family

During the first 20 days of the month, you will be immersed in work, and your personal life might be on the back burner.

However, those who are totally focused on family or romantic relationships would be wise to keep their eyes open during the second 10 days of June.

During this time, you may experience serious troubles with your loved one, who might ignore your needs, offend you, and appear unaware of everything you are willing to do for him or her. That goes for whether you divorced long ago, are in the middle of divorcing, or your current relationship simply leaves a lot to be desired.

Couples who get along will overcome a series of difficulties together, and thanks to your wisdom and undying love, your partner will be able to get through this rough period.

During all of the potential clashes this month, seek support from a circle of friends. Only they can influence your better half. The best time for this is during the last 10 days of June.

Health

This month, you are full of energy, but during the second 10 days of June, be careful when traveling and driving, especially from June 10-13.

July

New York Time			London Time		
Calendar Day	Lunar Day	Lunar Day Start Time	Calendar Day	Lunar Day	Lunar Day Start Time
01/07/24	25	1.56 AM	01/07/24	25	1.30 AM
02/07/24	26	2.34 AM	02/07/24	26	1.58 AM
03/07/24	27	3.17 AM	03/07/24	27	2.32 AM
04/07/24	28	4.07 AM	04/07/24	28	3.16 AM
05/07/24	29	5.03 AM	05/07/24	29	4.10 AM
05/07/24	1	6.59 PM	05/07/24	1	11.59 PM
06/07/24	2	6.04 AM	06/07/24	2	5.13 AM
07/07/24	3	7.07 AM	07/07/24	3	6.21 AM
08/07/24	4	8.10 AM	08/07/24	4	7.32 AM
09/07/24	5	9.11 AM	09/07/24	5	8.42 AM
10/07/24	6	10.11 AM	10/07/24	6	9.50 AM
11/07/24	7	11.09 AM	11/07/24	7	10.57 AM
12/07/24	8	12.07 PM	12/07/24	8	12.03 PM
13/07/24	9	1.05 PM	13/07/24	9	1.09 PM
14/07/24	10	2.04 PM	14/07/24	10	2.16 PM
15/07/24	11	3.04 PM	15/07/24	11	3.24 PM
16/07/24	12	4.06 PM	16/07/24	12	4.34 PM
17/07/24	13	5.09 PM	17/07/24	13	5.43 PM
18/07/24	14	6.10 PM	18/07/24	14	6.48 PM
19/07/24	15	7.07 PM	19/07/24	15	7.46 PM
20/07/24	16	7.58 PM	20/07/24	16	8.35 PM
21/07/24	17	8.42 PM	21/07/24	17	9.13 PM
22/07/24	18	9.21 PM	22/07/24	18	9.44 PM
23/07/24	19	9.55 PM	23/07/24	19	10.09 PM
24/07/24	20	10.26 PM	24/07/24	20	10.31 PM
25/07/24	21	10.56 PM	25/07/24	21	10.52 PM
26/07/24	22	11.26 PM	26/07/24	22	11.12 PM
27/07/24	23	11.58 PM	27/07/24	23	11.35 PM
29/07/24	24	12.34 AM	29/07/24	24	12.01 AM
30/07/24	25	1.15 AM	30/07/24	25	12.33 AM
31/07/24	26	2.03 AM	31/07/24	26	1.14 AM

You can find the description of each lunar day in the chapter "A Guide to The Moon Cycle and Lunar Days"

The big decisions you previously made are starting to bear out. This month, you will see that happen at work, with your finances, and your personal relationships.

Work

In July, your troubles from last month will have been resolved, and a difficult relationship with business partners will now bring you to a positive dialogue. In that case, your friends or someone highly placed may act as an intermediary. Keep in mind as well that a lean compromise is better than a fat lawsuit – that goes for both you and your adversaries. However, any harmony you achieve here might be delicate, and any arguments might repeat themselves in the near future. So do everything in your power and prepare stable ground for your upcoming clashes.

Your relationship with colleagues from other cities or abroad is now actively developing. In addition to former partners, you will also be dealing with new acquaintances, who will give you the support you need, when you need it.

Any trips planned for July will turn out successfully and help promote your projects at a new level of development and prosperity.

Employees will be able to strengthen their position, as well. If you recently began a new job, right now, the time has come to make your voice heard on your team. If you are looking for a new place for your talents, you might talk to old connections, who will be able to help you get what you want.

Money

Your financial position is looking stable, overall. Your expenses are in line with your income, and closer to the end of the month, you will still be in the black.

Love and family

Your personal life isn't easy, but it's on an extremely exciting and positive streak right now. Severe Saturn is firmly in the sector of the sky responsible for love, long-term relationships, and marriages, which has many Virgos separating or pulling away from their partners. But Saturn is now turning to another, lighter side, which will give many an opportunity to reconsider and possibly reconcile. The anger and rage will fade away, and for the first time in many months, you will be able to really feel things and reevaluate.

You might benefit from support from your friends or your shared children, and events that bring you together during this wonderful summer month.

Single people might spend time with new friends, and the warm connections and atmosphere might lead to something more. There are many opportunities this month, and it's up to you to take advantage of them.

Health

During the first 20 days of July, you are feeling fairly energetic and have no reason to fear falling ill. Your charm, sparkling sense of humor, and clear mind will grow even stronger. During the last 10 days of the month, you might feel a bit of fatigue from all of the activities this month.

July is a time for relaxation, and the stars urge you to take advantage of that.

August

New York Time			London Time		
Calendar Day	Lunar Day	Lunar Day Start Time	Calendar Day	Lunar Day	Lunar Day Start Time
01/08/24	27	2.56 AM	01/08/24	27	2.03 AM
02/08/24	28	3.54 AM	02/08/24	28	3.02 AM
03/08/24	29	4.56 AM	03/08/24	29	4.08 AM
04/08/24	30	5.58 AM	04/08/24	30	5.17 AM
04/08/24	1	7.14 AM	04/08/24	1	12.14 PM
05/08/24	2	7.00 AM	05/08/24	2	6.27 AM
06/08/24	3	8.00 AM	06/08/24	3	7.36 AM
07/08/24	4	8.59 AM	07/08/24	4	8.43 AM
08/08/24	5	9.57 AM	08/08/24	5	9.50 AM
09/08/24	6	10.55 AM	09/08/24	6	10.55 AM
10/08/24	7	11.53 AM	10/08/24	7	12.02 PM
11/08/24	8	12.52 PM	11/08/24	8	1.09 PM
12/08/24	9	1.52 PM	12/08/24	9	2.17 PM
13/08/24	10	2.54 PM	13/08/24	10	3.25 PM
14/08/24	11	3.54 PM	14/08/24	11	4.31 PM
15/08/24	12	4.52 PM	15/08/24	12	5.32 PM
16/08/24	13	5.46 PM	16/08/24	13	6.21 PM
17/08/24	14	6.33 PM	17/08/24	14	7.07 PM
18/08/24	15	7.15 PM	18/08/24	15	7.42 PM
19/08/24	16	7.51 PM	19/08/24	16	8.10 PM
20/08/24	17	8.24 PM	20/08/24	17	8.33 PM
21/08/24	18	8.56 PM	21/08/24	18	8.55 PM
22/08/24	19	9.27 PM	22/08/24	19	9.17 PM
23/08/24	20	9.59 PM	23/08/24	20	9.39 PM
24/08/24	21	10.35 PM	24/08/24	21	10.05 PM
25/08/24	22	11.15 PM	25/08/24	22	10.35 PM
27/08/24	23	12.00 AM	26/08/24	23	11.13 PM
28/08/24	24	12.52 AM	28/08/24	24	12.00 AM
29/08/24	25	1.48 AM	29/08/24	25	12.56 AM
30/08/24	26	2.48 AM	30/08/24	26	1.59 AM
31/08/24	27	3.50 AM	31/08/24	27	3.07 AM

You can find the description of each lunar day in the chapter "A Guide to The Moon Cycle and Lunar Days"

August will not exactly be the most successful month of the year for you. You may face opposition, clashing opinions, and even outright aggression. This may be work-related, or possibly something in your personal life. Get ready to defend yourself on all fronts!

Work

There is no doubt about your professional success, but not everyone is pleased with it.

In August, you may face aggressive business partners, who have an eye on your business and its future development.

The most difficult time will be after August 15, but things will be brewing in the first half of the month.

You may also have a challenging relationship with colleagues from other cities or abroad. Your partners from far away want to remind you of their position and you will have to deal with this in August, as well as into September. You may also have secret enemies, who will start rumors about you. This is true for all Virgos, regardless of what field they work in.

Employees should be adaptable and put all efforts into resolving conflict through diplomatic means. There is also another alternative – many Virgos will take some vacation time this month and focus on themselves. You will certainly have an opportunity to do just that.

Money

Naturally, with the way things are going, you can expect money trouble. However, you can count on a small sum on August 8, 9, 18, 19, 26, and 27.

Love and family

Your personal life is difficult, especially if you have had trouble here before. After several weeks going your way, you will see several problems appear, and you will be grappling with them until mid-September.

Divorcing and separated couples might return to the past, falling back into old patterns and conflicts.

Stable partners will also feel tension in their relationship. You and your partner will have seriously clashing views or opinions on something, which might lead to serious arguments or be a major factor as things cool off between you.

Things will be compounded by an unstable legal situation, especially if you recently moved abroad.

Health

This month, you are noticeably less energetic than you have been, and that often leads to the reappearance of old illnesses or new health problems. Be careful when traveling and driving.

September

New York Time			London Time		
Calendar Day	Lunar Day	Lunar Day Start Time	Calendar Day	Lunar Day	Lunar Day Start Time
01/09/24	28	4.51 AM	01/09/24	28	4.16 AM
02/09/24	29	5.52 AM	02/09/24	29	5.25 AM
02/09/24	1	9.56 PM	03/09/24	1	2.56 AM
03/09/24	2	6.51 AM	03/09/24	2	6.32 AM
04/09/24	3	7.49 AM	04/09/24	3	7.39 AM
05/09/24	4	8.47 AM	05/09/24	4	8.45 AM
06/09/24	5	9.45 AM	06/09/24	5	9.51 AM
07/09/24	6	10.43 AM	07/09/24	6	10.57 AM
08/09/24	7	11.43 AM	08/09/24	7	12.04 PM
09/09/24	8	12.42 PM	09/09/24	8	1.11 PM
10/09/24	9	1.42 PM	10/09/24	9	2.17 PM
11/09/24	10	2.40 PM	11/09/24	10	3.19 PM
12/09/24	11	3.34 PM	12/09/24	11	4.14 PM
13/09/24	12	4.23 PM	13/09/24	12	5.00 PM
14/09/24	13	5.06 PM	14/09/24	13	5.37 PM
15/09/24	14	5.44 PM	15/09/24	14	6.07 PM
16/09/24	15	6.19 PM	16/09/24	15	6.33 PM
17/09/24	16	6.51 PM	17/09/24	16	6.56 PM
18/09/24	17	7.23 PM	18/09/24	17	7.18 PM
19/09/24	18	7.56 PM	19/09/24	18	7.40 PM
20/09/24	19	8.31 PM	20/09/24	19	8.05 PM
21/09/24	20	9.11 PM	21/09/24	20	8.35 PM
22/09/24	21	9.56 PM	22/09/24	21	9.11 PM
23/09/24	22	10.46 PM	23/09/24	22	9.55 PM
24/09/24	23	11.42 PM	24/09/24	23	10.49 PM
26/09/24	24	12.42 AM	25/09/24	24	11.51 PM
27/09/24	25	1.44 AM	27/09/24	25	12.58 AM
28/09/24	26	2.45 AM	28/09/24	26	2.07 AM
29/09/24	27	3.45 AM	29/09/24	27	3.16 AM
30/09/24	28	4.44 AM	30/09/24	28	4.23 AM

You can find the description of each lunar day in the chapter "A Guide to The Moon Cycle and Lunar Days"

In September, you will have to face others' opinions, and they are likely to clash with your own. In some cases, that may happen at work, and in others, your personal life.

Work

Virgos who are part of the working world will spend over half of September grappling with problems that began in August. That will probably include disagreements with partners over shared business, as well as future business development.

You might also have to address each partner's role, job descriptions, and financial investments in your shared endeavor.

Everyone will have their own opinion here, so there is no avoiding disputes. Your adversaries will dig into their position, but you're plenty stubborn yourself, so you may have finally met your match.

The first 20 days of September will be far more difficult here, and things will start to slowly resolve themselves after that. You may have to lean on old friends to act as intermediaries, but things aren't so simple. A few months down the road, this story will repeat itself.

Your relationship with colleagues in other cities or abroad is coming along as you had planned. That is thanks to your efforts alone, but you can be sure they will pay off in dividends.

Employees will face competition and ill will from foes hoping to minimize their contributions. Be attentive when you talk to management. Demand less of them and refrain from asking any questions, even if you know you are right. Keep your head down, do your work, and remember that you will be highly appreciated and in demand.

Money

Venus, the planet of small victories, will spend nearly all of September in the financial sector of your sky, which means that you will not find yourself in the red. Expect to receive the largest amounts of money on September 5, 6, 14-16, and 22-24.

Love and family

If your interests are more aligned with your personal life, and if you have few blemishes in your past, you might expect a variety of problems to come your way this month. After a relatively peaceful July and difficult August, September is looking like a turbulent time. Though you can count on full or partial financial victories, the moral side of the equation will be very difficult. Your partner might become harsh or unyielding, appear that they no longer have feelings for you, or the fire has simply gone out.

Alternatively, a loved one will face problems, and that may be irritating or cause you tension.

Those who are moving somewhere far away might successfully manage challenges that cropped up in August.

Health

This month, you will have more strength, which means you will be able to successfully grapple with all of September's challenges.

October

New York Time			London Time		
Calendar Day	Lunar Day	Lunar Day Start Time	Calendar Day	Lunar Day	Lunar Day Start Time
01/10/24	29	5.42 AM	01/10/24	29	5.30 AM
02/10/24	30	6.40 AM	02/10/24	30	6.35 AM
02/10/24	1	1.50 PM	02/10/24	1	7.50 PM
03/10/24	2	6.38 AM	03/10/24	2	7.41 AM
04/10/24	3	7.36 AM	04/10/24	3	8.48 AM
05/10/24	4	8.36 AM	05/10/24	4	9.55 AM
06/10/24	5	9.35 AM	06/10/24	5	11.02 AM
07/10/24	6	10.35 AM	07/10/24	6	12.08 PM
08/10/24	7	11.32 AM	08/10/24	7	1.11 PM
09/10/24	8	12.26 PM	09/10/24	8	2.07 PM
10/10/24	9	1.16 PM	10/10/24	9	2.55 PM
11/10/24	10	2.00 PM	11/10/24	10	3.34 PM
12/10/24	11	2.39 PM	12/10/24	11	4.06 PM
13/10/24	12	3.14 PM	13/10/24	12	4.33 PM
14/10/24	13	3.46 PM	14/10/24	13	4.56 PM
15/10/24	14	4.18 PM	15/10/24	14	5.18 PM
16/10/24	15	4.50 PM	16/10/24	15	5.40 PM
17/10/24	16	5.24 PM	17/10/24	16	6.03 PM
18/10/24	17	6.02 PM	18/10/24	17	6.31 PM
19/10/24	18	6.46 PM	19/10/24	18	7.04 PM
20/10/24	19	7.36 PM	20/10/24	19	7.46 PM
21/10/24	20	8.32 PM	21/10/24	20	8.38 PM
22/10/24	21	9.32 PM	22/10/24	21	9.39 PM
23/10/24	22	10.34 PM	23/10/24	22	10.47 PM
24/10/24	23	11.37 PM	24/10/24	23	11.56 PM
26/10/24	24	12.38 AM	26/10/24	24	1.06 AM
27/10/24	25	1.38 AM	27/10/24	25	1.14 AM
28/10/24	26	2.36 AM	28/10/24	26	2.20 AM
29/10/24	27	3.34 AM	29/10/24	27	3.26 AM
30/10/24	28	4.31 AM	30/10/24	28	4.32 AM
31/10/24	29	5.30 AM	31/10/24	29	5.38 AM

You can find the description of each lunar day in the chapter "A Guide to The Moon Cycle and Lunar Days"

You are in for a wonderful month! Your wishes will come true, and your spirit will feel calm. Times like this don't come very often, so take advantage of the stars' influence and do whatever you have in mind.

Work

When it comes to anything-work related, October is one of the best months of 2024! Things will move forward, and new projects and opportunities will come your way.

Business owners and managers will receive profits from work you completed earlier and lay plans for the future.

Employees can expect support from managers and a corresponding salary raise. You are likely to receive a new job offer with an enticing financial incentive.

Your relationship with colleagues from other cities is moving along the way you need it to. Here, you may find stability, though there might still be some trouble on the horizon. This month, however, you will be able to address it easily, by leveraging your sign's diplomatic skills.

Any trips planned for October will be successful, especially If they do not take place from October 15 to 17, when there is a high chance of accidents.

Money

The solar eclipse on October 2 will shed powerful light on the financial sector of your sky. That means that you will have more money, and this is a positive development that will continue into the future. You might even say that many Virgos will be on a golden streak when it comes to their income and material wealth.

Expect to receive the largest amounts on October 2, 3, 12, 13, 20, 21, and 29-31. Your expenses are not going anywhere, but they are well below your income, which is significantly higher.

Love and family

Your personal life is calming down. Divorced and separated couples might peacefully resolve difficult financial matters. Things will lean in your favor most likely when it comes to anything material.

The harsh mood of the second half of October can be smoothed over when you approach dialogue with tact and flexibility. This advice is valid for all Virgos, regardless of your marital status. Severe Saturn has dug into the sector of the sky responsible for long-term relationships and will make you pay for any mistakes you have made, either now or in the past.

If your partner is going through challenging times, it is worth supporting him or her in both words and deeds.

You are growing closer to relatives, and you might visit family members who live in other cities or abroad.

Your children will require attention and major spending right now, but that is not a problem. You can afford it all.

Health

In October, you are energetic enough, but it's not worth putting your body to the test. Lead a healthy lifestyle and everything will be just fine.

November

New York Time			London Time		
Calendar Day	Lunar Day	Lunar Day Start Time	Calendar Day	Lunar Day	Lunar Day Start Time
01/11/24	30	6.29 AM	01/11/24	30	6.45 AM
01/11/24	1	7.48 AM	01/11/24	1	12.48 PM
02/11/24	2	7.29 AM	02/11/24	2	7.53 AM
03/11/24	3	8.29 AM	03/11/24	3	9.00 AM
04/11/24	4	9.27 AM	04/11/24	4	10.04 AM
05/11/24	5	10.23 AM	05/11/24	5	11.03 AM
06/11/24	6	11.13 AM	06/11/24	6	11.53 AM
07/11/24	7	11.58 AM	07/11/24	7	12.34 PM
08/11/24	8	12.37 PM	08/11/24	8	1.08 PM
09/11/24	9	1.13 PM	09/11/24	9	1.35 PM
10/11/24	10	1.44 PM	10/11/24	10	1.58 PM
11/11/24	11	2.15 PM	11/11/24	11	2.20 PM
12/11/24	12	2.45 PM	12/11/24	12	2.40 PM
13/11/24	13	3.17 PM	13/11/24	13	3.02 PM
14/11/24	14	3.53 PM	14/11/24	14	3.27 PM
15/11/24	15	4.33 PM	15/11/24	15	3.57 PM
16/11/24	16	5.20 PM	16/11/24	16	4.35 PM
17/11/24	17	6.15 PM	17/11/24	17	5.22 PM
18/11/24	18	7.15 PM	18/11/24	18	6.21 PM
19/11/24	19	8.19 PM	19/11/24	19	7.28 PM
20/11/24	20	9.23 PM	20/11/24	20	8.39 PM
21/11/24	21	10.27 PM	21/11/24	21	9.51 PM
22/11/24	22	11.28 PM	22/11/24	22	11.01 PM
24/11/24	23	12.27 AM	24/11/24	23	12.09 AM
25/11/24	24	1.25 AM	25/11/24	24	1.15 AM
26/11/24	25	2.23 AM	26/11/24	25	2.21 AM
27/11/24	26	3.21 AM	27/11/24	26	3.27 AM
28/11/24	27	4.20 AM	28/11/24	27	4.33 AM
29/11/24	28	5.20 AM	29/11/24	28	5.41 AM
30/11/24	29	6.21 AM	30/11/24	29	6.49 AM

You can find the description of each lunar day in the chapter "A Guide to The Moon Cycle and Lunar Days"

November is a time of contrasts for you. There will not be any dark periods, but you can certainly expect alternating clouds and sunshine. There is not much you can do about this – c'est la vie!

Work

Your main task in November is to reconnect with business partners with whom your cooperation may have suffered over the last year. The positive steps you began in October will continue into November, but in some cases, you will have to turn to intermediaries to help smooth things over.

An attorney or perhaps a kind soul from your inner circle may play this role.

Your relationship with colleagues in other cities or abroad is coming along nicely, and you may hold promising negotiations or take a successful trip.

The difficulties this month might include some disagreements over real estate, land, or other major property. This situation might continue into December.

Employees should be careful when it comes to their job, and if you can, avoid arguments with management. Here, some tension and unpleasant interactions are inevitable.

Mid-November is a time of conflict, as is next month.

Money

Financially, November looks fairly neutral. Your income will be average, and your expenses will be low. You can count on receiving some money on November 8, 9, 16, 17, and 25-27.

Love and family

In many cases, the main events of November will take place in your personal life. Divorcing and separated couples might continue to argue over their joint property, especially real estate. In order to overcome these difficult issues, you will have to lean on relatives, old friends, or a well-wishing friend.

Your children will bring you joy, and they may serve as a bridge between couples who are fighting or already divorced.

You might take a trip, which will make your relationship stronger, as long as there is something left to fix.

Those who are moving to a faraway place might have difficulty securing a place to live, and here, the spanner in the works might be official government bodies and red tape.

Health

In November, your energy is high, and you have no reason to fear falling ill.

December

New York Time		
Calendar Day	Lunar Day	Lunar Day Start Time
1	01/12/24	1.22 AM
2	01/12/24	7.21 AM
3	02/12/24	8.18 AM
4	03/12/24	9.11 AM
5	04/12/24	9.58 AM
6	05/12/24	10.39 AM
7	06/12/24	11.15 AM
8	07/12/24	11.47 AM
9	08/12/24	12.17 PM
10	09/12/24	12.46 PM
11	10/12/24	1.16 PM
12	11/12/24	1.48 PM
13	12/12/24	2.25 PM
14	13/12/24	3.07 PM
15	14/12/24	3.58 PM
16	15/12/24	4.55 PM
17	16/12/24	5.58 PM
18	17/12/24	7.04 PM
19	18/12/24	8.10 PM
20	19/12/24	9.13 PM
21	20/12/24	10.15 PM
22	21/12/24	11.14 PM
23	23/12/24	12.12 AM
24	24/12/24	1.10 AM
25	25/12/24	2.09 AM
26	26/12/24	3.08 AM
27	27/12/24	4.08 AM
28	28/12/24	5.09 AM
29	29/12/24	6.08 AM
30	30/12/24	7.04 AM
1	30/12/24	5.27 PM
2	31/12/24	7.54 AM

London Time		
Calendar Day	Lunar Day	Lunar Day Start Time
01/12/24	1	6.22 AM
01/12/24	2	7.56 AM
02/12/24	3	8.57 AM
03/12/24	4	9.51 AM
04/12/24	5	10.35 AM
05/12/24	6	11.11 AM
06/12/24	7	11.40 AM
07/12/24	8	12.04 PM
08/12/24	9	12.25 PM
09/12/24	10	12.45 PM
10/12/24	11	1.05 PM
11/12/24	12	1.28 PM
12/12/24	13	1.54 PM
13/12/24	14	2.27 PM
14/12/24	15	3.08 PM
15/12/24	16	4.01 PM
16/12/24	17	5.05 PM
17/12/24	18	6.16 PM
18/12/24	19	7.29 PM
19/12/24	20	8.42 PM
20/12/24	21	9.52 PM
21/12/24	22	11.00 PM
23/12/24	23	12.07 AM
24/12/24	24	1.13 AM
25/12/24	25	2.19 AM
26/12/24	26	3.26 AM
27/12/24	27	4.34 AM
28/12/24	28	5.42 AM
29/12/24	29	6.46 AM
30/12/24	30	7.44 AM
30/12/24	1	10.27 PM
31/12/24	2	8.32 AM

You can find the description of each lunar day in the chapter "A Guide to The Moon Cycle and Lunar Days"

In December, your ruler, Mercury, will be in retrograde, which means you may be lacking in logic, patience, and inner calm – which also happen to be the very qualities you have always been known for. Remember that inner peace is the key to success in everything and do not give into emotional triggers.

Work

For Virgos who are part of the working world, December is a supremely difficult time.

You have been hoping for a breakthrough at work, and it may not happen quite the way you hoped. Instead, you might have to overcome challenges, and it won't be easy.

Business owners will once again clash with business partners, in a more acute version of the events from August. This time, you may disagree over your shared business, or perhaps how to divide it up. You might also run into trouble involving real estate. What's more, your work may come to the attention of various auditing agencies.

Employees might find themselves under an onslaught of criticism from management and office gossip. Any attempt to defend your side of the story will be counterproductive at best.

The stars recommend that you don't go into any open battlefield. Keep restraint and be cautious. At the very least, avoid any major decisions and hold tight. This applies to any Virgos, regardless of your field.

Money

When it comes to finances, December is relatively stable for you. You will have your regular earnings, and you can expect the largest sums to come in on December 6, 7, 14, 15, 23, and 24.

You still have expenses, and they may be related to either business or your personal life.

Love and family

This month, your personal life is no less important than work, but it is just as turbulent. After a temporary calm, spouses whose marriage is on the rocks will once again unleash war on one another. There is plenty of reason for this, including old grudges, and your better half's unwillingness to come to an understanding. Similar situations are likely for couples who are divorcing. In any case, the crux of the matter may be real estate or shared business (or how to divide it up). You will resolve this later on, but right now, there is no hope of a compromise.

Things might look difficult, and it is unpleasant, but some skeletons may be dragged out of the closet – either yours or your partner's. Perhaps you both have secrets that will come to light.

Health

Those who manage to escape any professional or personal strife might instead be hit with health problems. If you have suffered from various illnesses in the past, they might come roaring back. That may be facilitated by the tense, emotional backdrop this month, so take care of yourself, and remember that your nerves are behind any illness. Nothing is more important than your health, the rest will follow.

Virgo Description

Sign. Feminine, earth, mutable.

Ruler. Mercury.

Exaltation. Mercury.

Temperament. Melancholic, restrained, cold yet anxious.

Positive traits. Hard-working, business-minded, intelligent and with a great memory, teachable, methodical, punctual, pragmatic, neat, dignified.

Negative traits. Formal, petty, thoughtless, anxious, indecisive, self-centered, self-interested, cunning, prone to flattery, resentful, capricious, greedy, vain.

Weaknesses in the body. Gastro-intestinal tract, solar plexus, pylorus, duodenum, cecum, pancreas, spleen, liver, gallbladder, autonomic nervous system, abdominal cavity.

Metal. Brass.

Minerals. For a talisman- yellow agate and jasper. Generally- yellow sapphire, amber, citrine, chrysolite.

Numbers. 5, 10.

Day. Wednesday.

Colors. Bright green and yellow brown.

Virgo energy

Virgo's personality is colored by the energy of two planets – Mercury and Proserpina. Mercury impacts Virgos differently than it does Geminis, creating a calmer, less independent character. One might say that Proserpina's unhurried effect "slows down" Mercury's influence in Virgo. Virgo and Gemini share a brilliant intellect, but Proserpina is a powerful planet that unleashes the swirl of time. She endows her children with a sense of duty, punctuality, clarity, analytical abilities, a tendency to study the root cause of any problem, grow, and transition to a higher state. In order to that to happen, though, the conscious must work, which is what Virgo has been doing her entire life. Virgo is an Earth sign, making her a practical materialist guided by logic and common sense.

Astrological portrait of Virgo

Virgo is a sign associated with work, service, and duty. It is a sign that is capable of overcoming difficulties. This is why Virgo is always concerned with her health and does not hesitate to seek medical attention. Virgos are willing to work tirelessly for a good cause. Their goals are clear and real rather than simply theoretical ideals. Virgos do not build pies in the sky, and their work is what gives life meaning. Virgos cannot tolerate laziness in others and will not aid those who refuse to work.

Virgos analyze. They are rational, with perfectly developed logic. They have a clear mind, with few illusions about life or other people. Even in love, they are capable of seeing their partner's shortcomings and turn to various methods to correct them. This does not mean that Virgos are devoid of emotions or purely driven by logic, however. Virgo's feelings are there, but she will only rarely reveal them. Even love is first and foremost a duty to Virgo. If someone is truly in need, she will happily step up and do whatever is necessary. Virgo is an intellectual sign, and people born under it constantly strive for new knowledge. They are skilled at absorbing information and memorizing facts. This is why many Virgos are known to their friends as a walking encyclopedia.

They seem to know everything and give intelligent, practical advice on any topic. When asked about anything, it is as if they had a file in their head storing complete information on whatever topic is at hand, and they will not be satisfied until they have informed you of all of it. Virgo seeks knowledge to subdue matters with their mind – this is their great, cosmic task.

Virgos are thorough critics. But they are also extremely ambitious and painfully sensitive to any comments. If you start criticizing a Virgo, she will refute all of your arguments, and you will come to regret ever starting the discussion. Virgos are pedantic, judgmental, and calculated, and their ability to impose their opinion on others mean they are impervious to criticism.

Virgos may lack intuition and creativity. They have a need to touch and see everything with their own eyes, and it is difficult for them to grasp the abstract. They subject the entire world to excellent analysis but are less gifted at synthesizing what they perceive. This means that Virgos might have a tendency to miss the forest for the trees. Virgo's home is usually in perfect order. Less pleasant traits may be her coldness and emotional rigidity.

At her highest level, a Virgo is an erudite person full of information, but her greatest battle will be her own pedantry.

How to recognize a Virgo by appearance

A typical Virgo is a slender person with a somewhat disproportional figure. In adulthood, Virgo women may tend to lose more weight than they gain, and will stay in good physical shape, even in old age. Virgos have wide bones, and their facial expressions are serious and stern. They tend to be tall but are rarely excessively so. Their faces tend to be long, as is their nose, which thickens into the shape of a water droplet. Their features are thin and well-defined. They have small eyes. Virgos are modest and often shy, and do not seek to draw attention to themselves, even if they are famous.

Charting Virgo's Fate

In childhood and adolescence, Virgos will face great difficulties. Later, they will manage to reach stability and security. Virgo builds her own happiness through decades of hard work and trial and error. Virgos tend to suffer a crisis in their personal life between the ages of about 18 to 29. They may experience marriage followed by divorce. Perhaps it finding a suitable partner seems impossible. Virgos reach personal harmony rather late in life, after the age of 36, and in some cases, as late as 42.

A Guide to The Moon Cycle and Lunar Days

Since Ancient times, people have noticed that the moon has a strong influence on nature. Our Earth and everything living on it is a single living being, which is why the phases of the moon have such an effect on our health and mental state, and therefore, our lives. Remember Shakespeare and his description of Othello's jealousy in his famous tragedy:

"It is the very error of the moon, She comes more nearer Earth than she was wont And makes men mad."

If our inner rhythm is in harmony with that of the cosmos, we are able to achieve much more. People were aware of this a thousand years ago. The lunar calendar is ancient. We can find it among the ancient Sumerians (4000-3000 BC), the inhabitants of Mesopotamia, Native Americans, Hindus, and ancient Slavs. There is evidence that the Siberian Yakuts had a lunar calendar, as did the Malaysians.

Primitive tribes saw the moon as a source of fertility. Long before Christianity, the waxing moon was seen as favorable for planting new crops and starting a new business, for success and making money, while the waning moon was a sign that business would end.

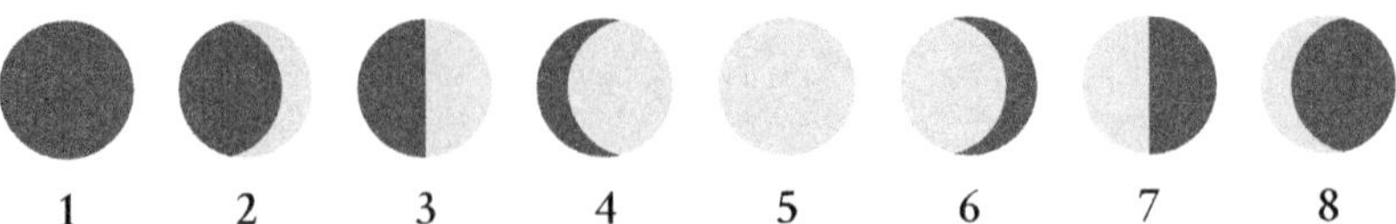

What are the phases of the moon?

- Phase 1 – new moon
- Phase 2 – waxing crescent moon
- Phase 3 – first quarter moon
- Phase 4 – waxing gibbous moon
- Phase 5 – full moon
- Phase 6 – waning gibbous moon
- Phase 7 – third quarter moon
- Phase 8 – waning crescent moon

To simplify things, we can divide the month into two phases:

- Waxing crescent moon - before the full moon
- Waning crescent moon - after the full moon

New Moon

We cannot see the new moon, as it is hidden. People might complain about feeling weak, mental imbalance, and fatigue. During this time, we want to avoid taking on too much or overdoing things. Generally, people are not very responsive and react poorly to requests, which is why it is best to look out for yourself, while not keeping your plate too full.

The new moon is a bad time for advertising – it will go unnoticed. It is not worth preparing any presentations, parties, or loud gatherings. People are feeling constrained, not very social, and sluggish.

This is also a less than ideal time for surgery, as your recovery will be slow, and the likelihood of medical error is high.

It is also difficult to get an accurate diagnosis during the new moon – diseases might seem to be hidden, and doctors might not see the real underlying cause of what ails you.

The new moon is also a bad time for dates, and sexual encounters may be dissatisfying and leave you feeling disappointed. Ancient astrologers did not advise planning a wedding night during the new moon.

Waxing Crescent Moon

It is easy to identify a waxing crescent moon. If you draw an imaginary line between the two "horns", you should see the letter P. The waxing moon is then divided into one and two quarters.

During the first quarter moon, we need to focus on planning – setting goals and thinking of how we will set about achieving them. However, it is still a good idea to hold back a bit and not overdo things. Energy levels are still low, though they are growing along with the moon. It is still a good idea to avoid any medical procedures during this time.

The second quarter is a time for bold, decisive action. Things will come easy, and there is a greater chance of a lucky break. This is a good time for weddings, especially if the moon will be in Libra, Cancer, or Taurus. Nevertheless, it is a good idea to put off any advertising activities and public speaking until closer to the full moon, if you can.

Full Moon

During the full moon, the Earth is located between the sun and the moon. During this time, the moon is round and fully illuminated. This takes place during days 14-16 of the lunar cycle.

During the full moon, many people feel more vigorous than usual. They are emotional, sociable, and actively seeking more contact, so this may be a good time for any celebrations.

However, be careful not to drink too much – you can relax to the point that you lose control, and the consequences of that can be very unpleasant. If you are able to stick to moderation, there is no better time for a party!

The full moon is also the best time for advertising, as not only will your campaign be widely seen, people will be apt to remember it.

The full moon is also a favorable time for dates, and during this time, people are at their most open, romantic, and willing to tell each other something important that might take their relationship to the next level of trust and understanding.

Moreover, during the full moon, people feel a surge of energy, which may lead to hyperactivity, restlessness, and insomnia.

It will be harder to keep your emotions in check. You might face conflicts with friends, disasters, and accidents. During the full moon, any surgeries are **not a good idea**, as the risk of complications and bleeding is on the rise. Plastic surgery is also a bad idea, as swelling and bruises might be much worse than in another lunar phase. At the same time, the full moon is a good time to get an accurate diagnosis.

During this time, try to limit your calories and liquid intake (especially if you deal with bloating and excess weight), as your body is absorbing both calories and liquids faster during the full moon, and it can be very difficult to get rid of the weight later on.

Waning Crescent Moon

The full moon is over, and a new phase is beginning – the waning moon. This is a quieter time, when all of the jobs you started earlier are being partly or entirely completed (it all depends on the speed and scale).

Surgery will turn out much better if it is performed during the waning moon. Your recovery will be faster, and the likelihood of complications is much lower. If you have any plans to lose weight, the waning moon is the best time to do that. This is also a good time for quitting bad habits, such as smoking or cursing.

The waning moon can also be divided into the third and fourth quarters.

Third quarter - this is a favorable period, and you are able to resolve a lot of problems without conflict. People are calming down and ready to listen and take in information, while still being active. However, this is not the best time to begin any major projects, especially if you are unsure if you will be able to complete them by the start of the new lunar month.

The third quarter is a good time to get married, especially if the moon is in Cancer, Taurus, or Libra.

Fourth quarter – This is the most passive period of the lunar cycle. You are not as strong as usual. Your energy is lagging. You will be tired until reaching a new beginning. The best thing you can do as the lunar cycle comes to an end is to get things in order, and avoid anything that might get in your way at work or in personal relationships. Examine your successes and failures.

Now, let's discuss the lunar days in greater detail. For centuries, people around the world have described the influence of lunar days, and modern astrologers only add to this work, as they compare old texts to modern life.

The 1st lunar day

The first lunar day is extremely important for the rest of the lunar month. This is a much-needed day to carefully plan your activities and lay the groundwork for the rest of the lunar month. Remember that the first lunar day is not a good day for major activities, but rather for sitting down and planning things.

Avoid conflicts on this day, unless you want them to overshadow the rest of the month. Try to see the positive side of things and imagine that the lunar month will bring you good things both at work and in love. The more vividly you can imagine this, the sooner your desires will come to fruition. Perhaps it would be a good idea to jot down plans that will bring you closer to achieving your dreams. This is the best time for both manifesting and making wishes!

This is also a favorable day when it comes to seeking a new job or starting an academic program.

It is fine to go out on a date on the first lunar day, but limit any sexual contact, as your energy levels are low, and you are likely to end up disappointed.

Getting married on the first lunar day is not recommended.

Avoid getting a haircut – there are many indications that cutting your hair on the first lunar day will have a negative effect on your health and life expectancy.

Under no circumstances should you undergo any major cosmetic procedures, including plastic surgery. Energy levels are low, your skin is dull and almost stagnant. The results will not live up to your expectations, and in the worst-case scenario, you will end up looking worse than before. It is common for cosmetic procedures performed on this day to be disappointing or even useless. Even the best surgeons are less capable.

Your good dreams on the first lunar day foretell happiness and joy. Bad ones usually do not come true.

The 2nd lunar day

This is considered a lucky day, and is symbolized by a cornucopia. It is not an exaggeration to say that the second lunar day is a favorable time for both work and love. It is a time for action, and a great period to work on yourself, look for a new job, start something new, or complete any financial transaction, whether a sale or purchase. This is also a great time for creative and scientific insights, and a good time for any meeting – whether political or romantic.

Any romantic dates or sexual encounters during the second lunar day are unlikely to disappoint. This is also a good day for weddings or taking a trip with someone special.

The 7th lunar day

This is also a favorable lunar day, and it is symbolized by a fighting cock, which is an Avestan deity. Avoid any aggression on this day, and instead work on yourself, spend time at home or in nature. Avoid discussing the status of your relationship with anyone, arguing, or wishing bad things on anyone. Everything will come back to haunt you, remember, silence is golden.

Business negotiations and contracts will be successful. You can find support, sponsors, and people ready to help you in both words and deeds.

Lighten up with your colleagues and subordinates. Pay attention not only to their shortcomings, but also to their skills. This is a good day for reconciliation and creating both political and romantic unions.

The seventh lunar day is good for traveling, no matter how near or far from home.

It is also a favorable time for love and marriage.

Exercise moderately, and any plastic surgeries will go very smoothly, as long as the moon is not in Scorpio.

Dreams of this day may become a reality.

The 8th lunar day

The symbol for this day is a Phoenix, which symbolizes eternal rebirth and renewal, because this day is a great time for changes in all areas of your life. Your energy is likely to be high, and you want to do something new and unusual. This is a good time to look for a new job or begin studying something. Any out-of-the-box thinking is welcome, along with shaking things up a bit in order to improve your life.

However, avoid any financial transactions, as you may incur losses.

Avoid aggression. You can share your opinion by presenting well-founded arguments and facts, instead.

The phoenix rises from the ashes, so this is a good time to be careful with electrical appliances and fire in general. The risk of housefires is high.

Avoid any major financial transactions on the eighth day, as you may end up facing a series of complications. You can pay people their salaries, as this is unlikely to be a large sum.

This is a good day for weddings, but only if you and your future spouse are restless, creative souls and hope to achieve personal development through your marriage.

Any cosmetic procedures and plastic surgeries will go well today, as they are related to rebirth and renewal. Surgeons may find that they are true artists on this day!

You can try to change your hairstyle and get a fashionable haircut on this day.

You can trust your dreams seen on this day.

The 9th lunar day

The ninth lunar day is not particularly auspicious, and is even referred to as "Satan's" day. You may be overcome with doubt, suspicions, even depression and conflicts.

Your self-esteem will suffer, so don't overdo things physically, and avoid overeating or abusing alcohol.

This is a negative day for any business deals, travel, or financial transactions.

This is a particularly bad day for any events, so keep your head down at work and avoid any new initiatives.

It is better to avoid getting married on "Satan's" day, as the marriage will not last very long. Avoid sex, as well, but you can take care of your partner, listen them, and support them however they need.

Any cosmetic procedures will not have a lasting effect, and avoid any plastic surgery. A haircut will not turn out as you hoped.

Dreams of this day are usually prophetic.

The 10th lunar day

This is one of the luckiest days of the lunar month. It is symbolized by a spring, mushroom, or phallus. This is a time for starting a new business, learning new things, and creating.

The 10th lunar day is particularly lucky for business. Networking and financial transactions will be a success and bring hope. This is an ideal time for changing jobs, shifting your business tactics, and other renewals.

This is a perfect time for people in creative fields and those working in science, who may come up with incredible ideas that will bring many successful returns.

This is a very successful day for building a family and proposing marriage. This is a good time for celebrations and communication, so plan parties, meet with friends, and plan a romantic date.

One of the symbols for this day is a phallus, so sexual encounters are likely to be particularly satisfying.

The 10th lunar day is the best time to begin repairs, buying furniture, and items for home improvement.

You can exercise vigorously, and cosmetic procedures and plastic surgery will be very effective.

Dreams of this day will not come true.

The 11th lunar day

This is one of the best lunar days, and seen as the pinnacle of the lunar cycle. People are likely to be energetic, enthusiastic, and ready to move forward toward their goals.

The 11th lunar day is very successful for any financial transactions or business deals and meetings.

You might actively make yourself known, approach management to discuss a promotion, or look for a new job. This is an auspicious time for advertising campaigns, performances, and holding meetings.

Any trips planned will be a great success, whether near or far from home.

Romantic relationships are improving, sex is harmonious, and very desired.

Weddings held on this day will be fun, and the marriage will be a source of joy and happiness.

Exercise is a great idea, and you might even beat your own personal record.

This is an ideal time for any cosmetic procedures, but any more serious plastic surgeries might lead to a lot of bruising and swelling.

A haircut will turn out as you had hoped, and you can experiment a bit with your appearance.

You can ignore dreams of this day – usually they do not mean anything.

The 12th lunar day

This day is symbolized by the Grail and a heart. As we move closer to the full moon, our emotions are at their most open. During this time, if you ask someone for something, your request will be heeded. This is a day of faith, goodness, and divine revelations.

For business and financial transactions, this is not the most promising day. However, if you help others on this day, your good deeds are sure to come back to you.

This is a day for reconciliation, so do not try to explain your relationships, as no one is at fault, and it is better to focus on yourself, anyway.

Avoid weddings and sex on this day, but if you want to do what your partner asks, there is no better time.

Many may feel less than confident and cheerful during this day, so take it easy when working out. Avoid overeating, stay hydrated, and avoid alcohol.

The 12th lunar day is not the best for getting married or having sex, but the stars would welcome affection and a kind word.

Avoid getting a haircut, or any plastic surgeries. This is a neutral day for minor cosmetic procedures.

Nearly all dreams will come true.

The 13th lunar day

This day is symbolized by Samsara, the wheel of fate, which is very erratic and capable of moving in any direction. This is why the 13th lunar day is full of contradictions. In Indian traditions, this day is compared to a snake eating its own tail. This is a day for paying off old debts and returning to unfinished business.

Avoid beginning any new business on this day. It is preferable to finish old tasks and proofread your work. Information you receive on this day may not be reliable and must be verified.

It is worth resolving financial problems very carefully, and avoid arguments and conflict.

Do not change jobs on this day or go to a new place for the first time. Do not sit at home alone, though, go see old friends, parents, or older family members.

Minor cosmetic procedures are welcome on this day, but avoid any plastic surgery, as you may experience major swelling and bruising. Avoid any haircuts, too.

As a rule, all dreams will come true.

The 14th lunar day

It's a full moon! The 14th lunar day is one of the happiest, and it is symbolized by the trumpet. Pay attention – you may run into new, much-needed information. Networking will be successful, and you can confidently sign agreements, meet with people, and attend fun gatherings or other leisure activities. This is one of the best days for advertising, performances, and concerts, and those working in creative professions should keep this in mind, as should those who work in politics. Do not sit in place on this day – you need to get out and see others, make new connections, and try to be visible.

This is one of the best days for communication with and making requests from management, as your initiatives will be noticed and welcome. You might talk about a promotion, raise, or something similarly related to professional growth.

Couples will see their relationship is moving along well on this day, and it is also a good day for getting married.

The 17th lunar day

This day is represented by a vine and bell. It is a happy day and both successful and fun-filled. It is also a good time for negotiations, concluding small business deals, shaking up staffing, and creativity. However, you should keep in mind that the 17th day is only favorable for minor business, and you should avoid starting any major events.

Avoid any major financial transactions on this day. Do not give anyone money as a loan or borrow anything yourself, either.

Any travel, whether for business or pleasure, is likely to be a success.

The 17th day is a great time to get married, and an ideal day for dates. Any sexual encounters will bring you happiness and joy.

Avoid getting your hair cut on this day, but cosmetic procedures and plastic surgery will be a success. Women will look better than usual.

Your dreams are likely to come true in three days.

The 18th lunar day

This day is represented by a mirror. It is a difficult, and generally unpromising day, too. Just as the mirror reflects our imperfections back to us, we need to remember that moderation and modesty are key.

The 18th day is not a favorable time for any business meetings or financial transactions. You can, however work on jobs you already began. It is, however, a positive day for those who work in research or the creative fields.

Your motto of the day is to keep a cool head when it comes to your opportunities and the opportunities of those around you. This is relevant for both work and romantic relationships. It is not a good time to criticize others – any conflicts or arguments may lead to lasting consequences, which you do not need.

Avoid getting married on this day, as well as sexual encounters, which are likely to be disappointing. It is a good time to take a trip together, which will only be good for your relationship.

Avoid getting your hair cut, though this is a relatively neutral day for a haircut, which might turn out well, and though it will not exceed your expectations, it will also not leave you upset. Avoid any plastic surgeries.

Dreams on this day will come true.

The 19th lunar day

This is a very difficult day and it is represented by a spider. The energy is complicated, if not outright dangerous. Don't panic or get depressed, though – this is a test of your strength, and if you are able to hold onto all you have achieved. This is relevant for both work and love. On the 19th day, you should avoid taking any trips.

The energy of the 19th lunar day is very unfavorable for beginning any major projects, and business in general. Work on what you started earlier, get your affairs in order, think over your ideas and emotions, and check to make sure that everything you have done hitherto is living up to your expectations. Do not carry out any financial transactions or take out any loans – do not loan anyone else money, either. Do not ask your managers for anything as they are unlikely to listen to what you have to say, and make judgments instead.

This is a day when you might face outright deception, so do not take any risks and ignore rumors. Do not work on anything related to real estate or legal matters.

This is a very hard time for people with an unbalanced psyche, as they may experience sudden exacerbations or even suicidal ideations.

This is a very unlucky day to get married. Sexual encounters might be disappointing and significantly worsen your relationship.

Avoid any haircuts or cosmetic procedures or surgeries.

Your dreams of this day will come true.

The 20th lunar day

This is also a difficult day, though less so than the 19th. It is represented by an eagle. This is a good time to work on your own development and spiritual growth, by speaking to a psychologist or astrologer.

Avoid pride, anger, arrogance, and envy.

The 20th lunar day is a good time for people who are active and decisive. They will be able to easily overcome any obstacles, flying over them just like an eagle. If you have to overcome your own fears, you will be able to do so – don't limit yourself, and you will see that there is nothing to be afraid of. It is a good day for any financial transactions, signing contracts, and reaching agreements, as well as networking.

The 20th lunar day is a favorable time for those who work in the creative fields, as they will be able to dream up the idea that will open up a whole host of new possibilities. Avoid conflicts – they may ruin your relationship with a lot of people, and it will not be easy to come back from that.

This is a lucky day for getting married, but only if you have been with your partner for several years, now. Sexual encounters will not be particularly joyful, but they also will not cause you any problems.

Avoid getting your hair cut, but you can certainly get it styled. The 20th lunar day is a good day for those who are looking to lose weight. You will be able to do so quickly, and it will be easy for you to follow a diet.

Cosmetic procedures will be a success, as will any plastic surgeries.

Pay attention to dreams of this day as they are likely to come true.

The 21st lunar day

This is one of the most successful days of the lunar month, and it is symbolized by a herd of horses – imagine energy, strength, speed, and bravery. Everything you think up will happen quickly, and you will be able to easily overcome obstacles. A mare is not only brave but also an honest animal, so you will only experience this luck if you remember that honesty is always the best policy.

This is also a favorable day for business. Reaching new agreements and signing contracts, or dealing with foreign partners – it is all likely to be a success. Any financial issues will be resolved successfully.

Those in the creative world will be able to show off their talent and be recognized for their work. Anyone involved in the performing arts can expect success, luck, and recognition. A galloping herd of horses moves quickly, so you might transition to a new job, move to a new apartment, or go on a business trip or travel with your better half.

The 21st lunar day is one of the best to get married or have a sexual encounter.

This is a great time for athletes, hunters, and anyone who likes adventurous activities.

But for criminals and thieves, this is not a lucky or happy day – they will quickly be brought to justice.

Any haircuts or cosmetic procedures are likely to be a huge success and bring both beauty and happiness. You will recover quickly after any surgeries, perhaps without any swelling or bruising at all.

Dreams tend to not be reliable.

The 22nd lunar day

This day will be strange and contradictory. It is symbolized by the elephant Ganesha. According to Indian mythology, Ganesha is the patron saint of hidden knowledge. so this is a favorable day for anyone who is trying to learn more about the world and ready to find the truth, though this is often seen as a hopeless endeavor. This is a day for philosophers and wisemen and women. However, it is an inauspicious day for business, and unlikely to lead to resolving financial issues, signing contracts, agreements, or beginning new projects. You can expect trouble at work.

For creative people, and new employees, this is a successful day.

This is a good day for apologies and reconciliation.

Avoid getting married, though you can feel free to engage in sexual encounters.

For haircuts and cosmetic procedures, this is a fantastic day. Surgeries will also turn out, as long as the moon is not in Scorpio.

Dreams will come true.

The 23rd lunar day

This is a challenging day represented by a crocodile, which is a very aggressive animal. This is a day of strong energy, but it is also adventurous and tough. Your main task is to focus your energy in the right direction. There may be accidents, arguments, conflicts, fights, and violence, which is why it is important to strive for balance and calm.

Keep a close eye on your surroundings – there may be traitors or people who do not wish you well, so be careful.

However, this is still a favorable day for business – many problems will be resolved successfully. You are able to sign contracts and receive credit successfully, as long as you remain active and decisive in what you do.

This is not a day for changing jobs or working on real estate transactions or legal proceedings. This is not a favorable day for traveling, no matter how near or far you plan on going.

This is not a promising day to get married – things may end in conflict, if not an all-out brawl.

Sexual relations are not off the table, as long as the couple trusts one another.

Haircuts or cosmetic procedures will not turn out as you had hoped, so avoid them.

Dreams during this lunar day usually mean something opposite of what awaits you, so you can disregard them.

The 24th lunar day

This is a neutral, calm day that is symbolized by a bear. It is favorable for forgiveness and reconciliation.

This is also a good day for learning new things, reading, self-development, and taking time to relax in nature.

This is a great day for any type of financial activity, conferences, academic meetings, and faraway travel.

The 24th lunar day is a good time for love and getting married, as any marriage will be strong and lasting.

Cosmetic procedures and plastic surgery will be a success, and you can expect a speedy recovery.

Avoid getting a haircut on this day, however, as your hair will likely thin and grow back slowly.

Dreams of this lunar day are usually connected with your personal life.

The 25th lunar day

This is still another quiet day, symbolized by a turtle.

Just like a turtle, this is not a day to rush, and it is best to sit down and take stock of your life. This is a good time for resolving any personal problems, as the moon's energy makes it possible for you to calm down and find the right path.

This is also not a bad day for business. It is believed that any business you begin on this day is sure to be a success. This is especially the case for trade and any monetary activities.

The 25th lunar day is not a good day to get married, especially if the couple is very young.

This is a neutral day for sexual encounters, as the moon is waning, energy is low, so the decision is yours.

Avoid any cosmetic procedures, except those for cleansing your skin. This is not a favorable day for haircuts or plastic surgery – unless the moon is in Libra or Leo.

You can have a prophetic dream on this day.

The 26th lunar day

The 26th lunar day is full of contradictions and complicated. It is represented by a toad.

It is not time to start or take on something new, as nothing good will come of it. Avoid any major purchases, as you will later come to see that your money was wasted. The best thing you can do on this day is stay at home and watch a good movie or read a good book.

Avoid traveling on this day, as it may not turn out well.

The 26th lunar day is a negative day for any business negotiations and starting new businesses. Do not complete any business deals or financial transactions. Your colleagues may be arguing, and your managers may be dissatisfied. But if you have decided to leave your job, there is no better time to do so.

This is not a good day to get married, as both partners' expectations may fall flat, and they will soon be disappointed.

The waning moon carries a negative charge, so avoid any haircuts and surgeries, though you can get cosmetic procedures if they are relatively minor.

Your dreams will come true.

The 27th lunar day

The 27th lunar day is one of the best days of the month, and it is represented by a ship. You can boldly start any new business, which is sure to be promising. This is a great day for students, teachers, and learning new things. Any information that comes to you on this day may be extremely valuable and useful to you.

The 27th day is good for communication and travel, whether near or far from home, and no matter whether it is for work or pleasure.

This is also a good day for any professional activities or financial transactions. If there are people around you who need help, you must support them, as your good deeds will come back 100-fold.

Romantic dates will go well, though any weddings should be quiet and subdued. This is a particularly good day for older couples or second marriages.

The waning moon means that hair will grow back very slowly, but in general, you can expect a haircut to turn out well. This is a great day for plastic surgery or cosmetic procedures, as the results will be pleasing, and you will have a speedy recovery, without any bruising or swelling, most of the time.

However, beware if the moon is in Scorpio on this day – that is not a good omen for any plastic surgery.

Do not pay any attention to dreams on this day.

The 28th lunar day

This is another favorable day in the waning moon cycle, and it is represented by a lotus. This is a day of wisdom and spiritual awakening. If possible, spend part of the day in nature. It is important to take stock of the last month and decide what you need to do during its two remaining days.

This is a good time for any career development, changing jobs, conducting business, decision-making, and signing agreements, as well as going on a trip. You might conclude any business deal, hold negotiations, work with money and securities.

This is also a good day for any repairs or improvements around your home or apartment.

Any weddings today should be subdued and modest, and restricted to family members only. A loud, raucous wedding might not turn out very well.

Your hair will grow slowly, but any haircuts will turn out very elegant and stylish. Cosmetic procedures and surgeries are not contraindicated. You will recover quickly with little bruising and swelling.

Do not take any dreams too seriously.

The 29th lunar day

This is one of the most difficult days of the lunar month, and it is considered a Satanic day, unlucky for everyone and everything. It is symbolized by an octopus.

This is a dark day, and many will feel melancholy, depression, and a desire to simply be left alone. This is a day full of conflict and injuries, so be careful everywhere and with everyone. If you can, avoid any travel, and be particularly careful when handling any sharp objects. Do not engage in any business negotiations, sign any contracts, or take part in any networking.

Astrologers believe that anything you start on this day will completely fall apart. For once and for all, get rid of things that are impeding you from living your life. This is a good time to avoid people who you do find unpleasant.

This is also a time for fasting and limitations for everyone. Do not hold any celebrations, weddings, or have sexual relations – these events may not turn out as you hoped, and instead bring you nothing but suffering and strife.

Avoid getting a haircut, as well, as it will not make you look more beautiful and your hair will come back lifeless and dull. Cosmetic procedures can go ahead, but avoid any surgeries.

Dreams are likely to be true.

The 30th lunar day

There is not always a 30th lunar day, as some lunar months have only 29 days. This day is represented by a swan. The 30th lunar day is usually very short, and sometimes, it lasts less than an hour. This is a time for forgiveness and calm.

You might take stock of the last month, while also avoiding anything you do not need around you. Pay back loans, make donations, reconcile with those who recently offended you, and stop speaking to people who cause you suffering.

This is a good time for tying up loose ends, and many astrologers believe that it is also a good day to start new business.

However, avoid celebrations or weddings on this day. Spouses will either not live long, or they will quickly grow apart.

Do not get a haircut on this day, though cosmetic procedures are possible, as long as you avoid any surgeries.

Dreams promise happiness and should come true.

A Guide to Zodiac Compatibility

Often, when we meet a person, we get a feeling that they are good and we take an instant liking to them. Another person, however, gives us immediate feelings of distrust, fear and hostility. Is there an astrological reason why people say that 'the first impression is the most accurate'? How can we detect those who will bring us nothing but trouble and unhappiness?

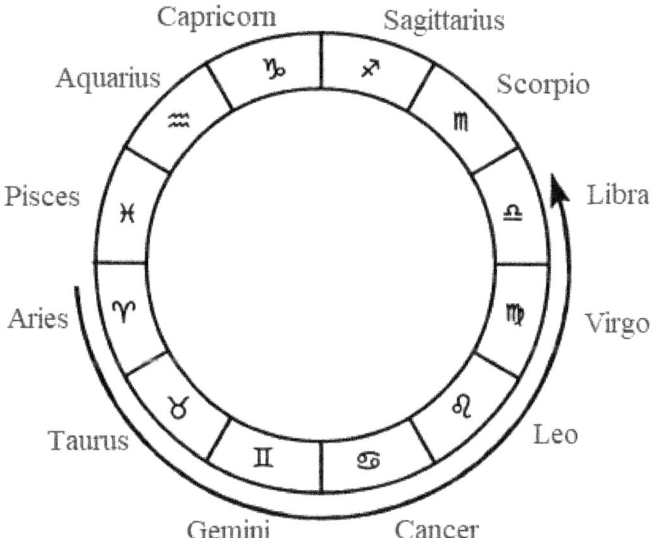

Without going too deeply into astrological subtleties unfamiliar to some readers, it is possible to determine the traits according to which friendship, love or business relationships will develop.

Let's begin with problematic relationships - our most difficult are with our **8th sign**. For example, for Aries the 8th sign is Scorpio, for Taurus it is Sagittarius and so on. Finding your 8th sign is easy; assume your own sign to be first (see above Figure) and then move eight signs counter clockwise around the Zodiac circle. This is also how the other signs (fourth, ninth and so on) that we mention are to be found.

Ancient astrologers variously referred to the 8th sign as the symbol of death, of destruction, of fated love or unfathomable attraction. In astrological terms, this pair is called 'master and slave' or 'boa constrictor and rabbit', with the role of 'master' or 'boa constrictor' being played by our 8th sign.

This relationship is especially difficult for politicians and business people.

We can take the example of a recent political confrontation in the USA. Hilary Clinton is a Scorpio while Donald Trump is a Gemini - her 8th sign. Even though many were certain that Clinton would be elected President, she lost.

To take another example, Hitler was a Taurus and his opponents – Stalin and Churchill - were both of his 8th sign, Sagittarius. The result of their confrontation is well known. Interestingly, the Russian Marshals who dealt crushing military blows to Hitler and so helped end the Third Reich - Konstantin Rokossovsky and Georgy Zhukov - were also Sagittarian, Hitler's 8th sign.

In another historical illustration, Lenin was also a Taurus. Stalin was of Lenin's 8th sign and was ultimately responsible for the downfall and possibly death of his one-time comrade-in-arms.

Business ties with those of our 8th sign are hazardous as they ultimately lead to stress and loss; both financial and moral. So, do not tangle with your 8th sign and never fight with it - your chances of winning are remote!

Such relationships are very interesting in terms of love and romance, however. We are magnetically attracted to our 8th sign and even though it may be very intense physically, it is very difficult for family life;

'Feeling bad when together, feeling worse when apart'.

As an example, let us take the famous lovers - George Sand who was Cancer and Alfred de Musset who was Sagittarius. Cancer is the 8th sign for Sagittarius, and the story of their crazy two-year love affair was the subject of much attention throughout France. Critics and writers were divided into 'Mussulist' and 'Sandist' camps; they debated fiercely about who was to blame for the sad ending to their love story - him or her. It's hard to imagine the energy needed to captivate the public for so long, but that energy was destructive for the couple. Passion raged in their hearts, but neither of them was able to comprehend their situation.

Georges Sand wrote to Musset, *"I don't love you anymore, and I will always adore you. I don't want you anymore, and I can't do without you. It seems that nothing but a heavenly lightning strike can heal me by destroying me. Good-bye! Stay or go, but don't say that I am not suffering. This is the only thing that can make me suffer even more, my love, my life, my blood! Go away, but kill me, leaving."* Musset replied only in brief, but its power surpassed Sand's tirade, *"When you embraced me, I felt something that is still bothering me, making it impossible for me to approach another woman."* These two people loved each other passionately and for two years lived together in a powder keg of passion, hatred and treachery.

When someone enters into a romantic liaison with their 8th sign, there will be no peace; indeed, these relationships are very attractive to those who enjoy the edgy, the borderline and, in the Dostoevsky style, the melodramatic. The first to lose interest in the relationship is, as a rule, the 8th sign.

If, by turn of fate, our child is born under our 8th sign, they will be very different from us and, in some ways, not live up to our expectations. It may be best to let them choose their own path.

In business and political relationships, the combination with our **12th sign** is also a complicated one.

We can take two political examples. Angela Merkel is a Cancer while Donald Trump is a Gemini - her 12th sign. This is why their relations are strained and complicated and we can even perhaps assume that the American president will achieve his political goals at her expense. Boris Yeltsin (Aquarius) was the 12th sign to Mikhail Gorbachev (Pisces) and it was Yeltsin who managed to dethrone the champion of Perestroika.

Even ancient astrologers noticed that our relationships with our 12th signs can never develop evenly; it is one of the most curious and problematic combinations. They are our hidden enemies and they seem to be digging a hole for us; they ingratiate themselves with us, discover our innermost secrets. As a result, we become bewildered and make mistakes when we deal with them. Among the Roman emperors murdered by members of their entourage, there was an interesting pattern - all the murderers were the 12th sign of the murdered.

We can also see this pernicious effect in Russian history: the German princess Alexandra (Gemini) married the last Russian Tsar Nicholas II (Taurus) - he was her 12th sign and brought her a tragic death. The wicked genius Grigory Rasputin (Cancer) made friends with Tsarina Alexandra, who was his 12th sign, and was murdered as a result of their odd friendship. The weakness of Nicholas II was exposed, and his authority reduced after the death of the economic and social reformer Pyotr Stolypin, who was his 12th sign. Thus, we see a chain of people whose downfall was brought about by their 12th sign.

So, it makes sense to be cautious of your 12th sign, especially if you have business ties. Usually, these people know much more about us than we want them to and they will often reveal our secrets for personal gain if it suits them. However, the outset of these relationships is, as a rule, quite normal - sometimes the two people will be friends, but sooner or later one will betray the other one or divulge a secret; inadvertently or not.

In terms of romantic relationships, our 12th sign is gentle, they take care of us and are tender towards us. They know our weaknesses well but accept them with understanding. It is they who guide us, although sometimes almost imperceptibly. Sexual attraction is usually strong.

For example, Meghan Markle is a Leo, the 12th sign for Prince Harry, who is a Virgo. Despite Queen Elizabeth II being lukewarm about the match, Harry's love was so strong that they did marry.

If a child is our 12th sign, it later becomes clear that they know all our secrets, even those that they are not supposed to know. It is very difficult to control them as they do everything in their own way.

Relations with our **7th sign** are also interesting. They are like our opposite; they have something to learn from us while we, in turn, have something to learn from them. This combination, in business and personal relationships, can be very positive and stimulating provided that both partners are quite intelligent and have high moral standards but if not, constant misunderstandings and challenges follow. Marriage or co-operation with the 7th sign can only exist as the union of two fully-fledged individuals and in this case love, significant business achievements and social success are possible.

However, the combination can be not only interesting, but also quite complicated.

An example is Angelina Jolie, a Gemini, and Brad Pitt, a Sagittarius. This is a typical bond with a 7th sign - it's lively and interesting, but rather stressful. Although such a couple may quarrel and even part from time to time, never do they lose interest in each other.

This may be why this combination is more stable in middle-age when there is an understanding of the true nature of marriage and partnership. In global, political terms, this suggests a state of eternal tension - a cold war - for example between Yeltsin (Aquarius) and Bill Clinton (Leo).

Relations with our **9th sign** are very good; they are our teacher and advisor - one who reveals things we are unaware of and our relationships with them very often involve travel or re-location. The combination can lead to spiritual growth and can be beneficial in terms of business.

Although, for example, Trump and Putin are political opponents, they can come to an understanding and even feel a certain sympathy for each other because Putin is a Libra while Trump is a Gemini, his 9th sign.

This union is also quite harmonious for conjugal and romantic relationships.

We treat our **3rd sign** somewhat condescendingly. They are like our younger siblings; we teach them and expect them to listen attentively. Our younger brothers and sisters are more often than not born under this sign. In terms of personal and sexual relationships, the union is not very inspiring and can end quickly, although this is not always the case. In terms of business, it is fairly average as it often connects partners from different cities or countries.

We treat our **5th sign** as a child and we must take care of them accordingly. The combination is not very good for business, however, since our 5th sign triumphs over us in terms of connections and finances, and thereby gives us very little in return save for love or sympathy. However, they are very good for family and romantic relationships, especially if the 5th sign is female. If a child is born as a 5th sign to their parents, their relationship will be a mutually smooth, loving and understanding one that lasts a lifetime.

Our **10th sign** is a born leader. Depending on the spiritual level of those involved, both pleasant and tense relations are possible; the relationship is often mutually beneficial in the good times but mutually disruptive in the bad times. In family relations, our 10th sign always tries to lead and will do so according to their intelligence and upbringing.

Our **4th sign** protects our home and can act as a sponsor to strengthen our financial or moral positions. Their advice should be heeded in all cases as it can be very effective, albeit very unobtrusive. If a woman takes this role, the relationship can be long and romantic, since all the spouse's wishes are usually met one way or another. Sometimes, such couples achieve great social success; for instance, Hilary Clinton, a Scorpio is the 4th sign to Bill Clinton, a Leo. On the other hand, if the husband is the 4th sign for his wife, he tends to be henpecked. There is often a strong sexual attraction. Our 4th sign can improve our living conditions and care for us in a parental way. If a child is our 4th sign, they are close to us and support us affectionately.

Relations with our **11th sign** are often either friendly or patronizing; we treat them reverently, while they treat us with friendly condescension. Sometimes, these relationships develop in an 'older brother' or 'high-ranking friend' sense; indeed, older brothers and sisters are often our 11th sign. In terms of personal and sexual relationships, our 11th sign is always inclined to enslave us. This tendency is most clearly manifested in such alliances as Capricorn and Pisces or Leo and Libra. A child who is the 11th sign to their parents will achieve greater success than their parents, but this will only make the parents proud.

Our **2nd sign** should bring us financial or other benefits; we receive a lot from them in both our business and our family life. In married couples, the 2nd sign usually looks after the financial situation for the benefit of the family. Sexual attraction is strong.

Our **6th sign** is our 'slave'; we always benefit from working with them and it's very difficult for them to escape our influence. In the event of hostility, especially if they have provoked the conflict, they receive a powerful retaliatory strike. In personal relations, we can almost destroy them by making them dance to our tune. For example, if a husband doesn't allow his wife to work or there are other adverse family circumstances, she gradually becomes lost as an individual despite being surrounded by care. This is the best-case scenario; worse outcomes are possible. Our 6th sign has a strong sexual attraction to us because we are the fatal 8th sign for them; we cool down quickly, however, and often make all kinds of demands. If the relationship with our 6th sign is a long one, there is a danger that routine, boredom and stagnation will ultimately destroy the relationship. A child born under our 6th sign needs particularly careful handling as they can feel fear or embarrassment when communicating with us. Their health often needs increased attention and we should also remember that they are very different from us emotionally.

Finally, we turn to relations with **our own sign**. Scorpio with Scorpio and Cancer with Cancer get along well, but in most other cases, however, our own sign is of little interest to us as it has a similar energy. Sometimes, this relationship can develop as a rivalry, either in business or in love.

There is another interesting detail - we are often attracted to one particular sign. For example, a man's wife and mistress often have the same sign. If there is confrontation between the two, the stronger character displaces the weaker one. As an example, Prince Charles is a Scorpio, while both Princess Diana and Camilla Parker Bowles were born under the sign of Cancer. Camilla was the more assertive and became dominant.

Of course, in order to draw any definitive conclusions, we need an individually prepared horoscope, but the above always, one way or another, manifests itself.

Love Description of Zodiac Signs

We know that human sexual behavior has been studied at length. Entire libraries have been written about it, with the aim of helping us understand ourselves and our partners. But is that even possible? It may not be; no matter how smart we are, when it comes to love and sex, there is always an infinite amount to learn. But we have to strive for perfection, and astrology, with its millennia of research, twelve astrological types, and twelve zodiac signs, may hold the key. Below, you will find a brief and accurate description of each zodiac sign's characteristics in love, for both men and women.

Men

ARIES

Aries men are not particularly deep or wise, but they make up for it in sincerity and loyalty. They are active, even aggressive lovers, but a hopeless romantic may be lurking just below the surface. Aries are often monogamous and chivalrous men, for whom there is only one woman (of course, in her absence, they can sleep around with no remorse). If the object of your affection is an Aries, be sure to give him a lot of sex, and remember that for an Aries, when it comes to sex, anything goes. Aries cannot stand women who are negative or disheveled. They need someone energetic, lively, and to feel exciting feelings of romance.

The best partner for an Aries is Cancer, Sagittarius, or Leo. Aquarius can also be a good match, but the relationship will be rather friendly in nature. Partnering with a Scorpio or Taurus will be difficult, but they can be stimulating lovers for an Aries. Virgos are good business contacts, but a poor match as lovers or spouses.

TAURUS

A typical Taurean man is warm, friendly, gentle, and passionate, even if he doesn't always show it. He is utterly captivated by the beauty of the female body, and can find inspiration in any woman. A Taurus has such excess physical and sexual prowess, that to him, sex is a way to relax and calm down. He is the most passionate and emotional lover of the Zodiac, but he expects his partner to take the initiative, and if she doesn't, he will easily find someone else. Taureans rarely divorce, and are true to the end – if not sexually, at least spiritually. They are secretive, keep their cards close, and may have secret lovers. If a Taurus does not feel a deep emotional connection with someone, he won't be shy to ask her friends for their number. He prefers a voluptuous figure over an athletic or skinny woman.

The best partners for a Taurus are Cancer, Virgo, Pisces, or Scorpio. Sagittarius can show a Taurus real delights in both body and spirit, but they are unlikely to make it down the aisle. They can have an interesting relationship with an Aquarius – these signs are very different, but sometimes can spend their lives together. They might initially feel attracted to an Aries, before rejecting her.

GEMINI

The typical Gemini man is easygoing and polite. He is calm, collected, and analytical. For a Gemini, passion is closely linked to intellect, to the point that they will try to find an explanation for their actions before carrying them out. But passion cannot be explained, which scares a Gemini, and they begin jumping from one extreme to the other. This is why you will find more bigamists among Geminis than any other sign of the Zodiac. Sometimes, Gemini men even have two families, or divorce and marry several times throughout the course of their lives. This may be because they simply can't let new and interesting experiences pass them by. A Gemini's wife or lover needs to be smart, quick, and always looking ahead. If she isn't, he will find a new object for his affection.

Aquarians, Libras, and Aries make good partners for a Gemini. A Sagittarius can be fascinating for him, but they will not marry before he reaches middle age, as both partners will be fickle while they are younger. A Gemini and Scorpio are likely to be a difficult match, and the Gemini will try to wriggle out of the Scorpio's tight embrace. A Taurus will be an exciting sex partner, but their partnership won't be for long, and the Taurus is often at fault.

CANCER

Cancers tend to be deep, emotional individuals, who are both sensitive and highly sexual. Their charm is almost mystical, and they know how to use it. Cancers may be the most promiscuous sign of the Zodiac, and open to absolutely anything in bed. Younger Cancers look for women who are more mature, as they are skilled lovers. As they age, they look for someone young enough to be their own daughter, and delight in taking on the role of a teacher. Cancers are devoted to building a family and an inviting home, but once they achieve that goal, they are likely to have a wandering eye. They will not seek moral justification, as they sincerely believe it is simply something everyone does. Their charm works in such a way that women are deeply convinced they are the most important love in a Cancer's life, and that circumstances are the only thing preventing them from being together. Remember that a Cancer man is a master manipulator, and will not be yours unless he is sure you have throngs of admirers. He loves feminine curves, and is turned on by exquisite fragrances. Cancers don't end things with old lovers, and often go back for a visit after a breakup. Another type of Cancer is rarer – a faithful friend, and up for anything in order to provide for his wife and children. He is patriotic and a responsible worker.

Scorpios, Pisces, and other Cancers are a good match. A Taurus can make for a lasting relationship, as both signs place great value on family and are able to get along with one another. A Sagittarius will result in fights and blowouts from the very beginning, followed by conflicts and breakups. The Sagittarius will suffer the most. Marriage to an Aries isn't off the table, but it won't last very long.

LEO

A typical Leo is handsome, proud, and vain, with a need to be the center of attention at all times. They often pretend to be virtuous, until they are able to actually master it. They crave flattery, and prefer women who comply and cater to them. Leos demand unconditional obedience, and constant approval. When a Leo is in love, he is fairly sexual, and capable of being devoted and faithful. Cheap love affairs are not his thing, and Leos are highly aware of how expensive it is to divorce. They make excellent fathers. A Leo's partner needs to look polished and well-dressed, and he will not tolerate either frumpiness or nerds.

Aries, Sagittarius, and Gemini make for good matches. Leos are often very beguiling to Libras; this is the most infamous astrological "master-slave" pairing. Leos are also inexplicably drawn to Pisces – this is the only sign capable of taming them. A Leo and Virgo will face a host of problems sooner or later, and they might be material in nature. The Virgo will attempt to conquer him, and if she does, a breakup is inevitable.

VIRGO

Virgo is a highly intellectual sign, who likes to take a step back and spend his time studying the big picture. But love inherently does not lend itself to analysis, and this can leave Virgos feeling perplexed. While Virgo is taking his time, studying the object of his affection, someone else will swoop in and take her away, leaving him bitterly disappointed. Perhaps for that reason, Virgos tend to marry late, but once they are married, they remain true, and hardly ever initiate divorce. In bed, they are modest and reserved, as they see sex as some sort of quirk of nature, designed solely for procreation. Most Virgos have a gifted sense of taste, hearing, and smell. They cannot tolerate pungent odors and can be squeamish; they believe their partners should always take pains to be very clean. Virgos usually hate over-the-top expressions of love, and are immune to sex as a mean s of control. Many Virgos are stingy and more appropriate as husbands than lovers. Male Virgos tend to be monogamous, though if they are unhappy or disappointed with their partner, they may begin to look for comfort elsewhere and often give in to drunkenness.

Taurus, Capricorn, and Scorpio make the best partners for a Virgo. They may feel inexplicable attraction for Aquarians. They will form friendships with Aries, but rarely will this couple make it down the aisle. With Leos, be careful – this sign is best as a lover, not a spouse.

LIBRA

Libra is a very complex, wishy-washy sign. They are constantly seeking perfection, which often leaves them in discord with the reality around them. Libra men are elegant and refined, and expect no less from their partner. Many Libras treat their partners like a beautiful work of art, and have trouble holding onto the object of their affection. They view love itself as a very abstract concept, and can get tired of the physical aspect of their relationship. They are much more drawn to intrigue and the chase- dreams, candlelit evenings, and other symbols of romance. A high percentage of Libra men are gay, and they view sex with other men as the more elite option. Even when Libras are unhappy in their marriages, they never divorce willingly. Their wives might leave them, however, or they might be taken away by a more decisive partner.

Aquarius and Gemini make the best matches for Libras. Libra can also easily control an independent Sagittarius, and can easily fall under the influence of a powerful and determined Leo, before putting all his strength and effort into breaking free. Relationships with Scorpios are difficult; they may become lovers, but will rarely marry.

SCORPIO

Though it is common to perceive Scorpios as incredibly sexual, they are, in fact, very unassuming, and never brag about their exploits. They will, however, be faithful and devoted to the right woman. The Scorpio man is taciturn, and you can't expect any tender words from him, but he will defend those he loves to the very end. Despite his outward control, Scorpio is very emotional; he needs and craves love, and is willing to fight for it. Scorpios are incredible lovers, and rather than leaving them tired, sex leaves them feeling energized. They are always sexy, even if they aren't particularly handsome. They are unconcerned with the ceremony of wooing you, and more focused on the act of love itself.

Expressive Cancers and gentle, amenable Pisces make the best partners. A Scorpio might also fall under the spell of a Virgo, who is adept at taking the lead. Sparks might fly between two Scorpios, or with a Taurus, who is perfect for a Scorpio in bed. Relationships with Libras, Sagittarians, and Aries are difficult.

SAGITTARIUS

Sagittarian men are lucky, curious, and gregarious. Younger Sagittarians are romantic, passionate, and burning with desire to experience every type of love. Sagittarius is a very idealistic sign, and in that search for perfection, they tend to flit from one partner to another, eventually forgetting what they were even looking for in the first place. A negative Sagittarius might have two or three relationships going on at once, assigning each partner a different day of the week. On the other hand, a positive Sagittarius will channel his powerful sexual energy into creativity, and take his career to new heights. Generally speaking, after multiple relationships and divorces, the Sagittarian man will conclude that his ideal marriage is one where his partner is willing to look the other way.

Aries and Leo make the best matches for a Sagittarius. He might fall under the spell of a Cancer, but would not be happy being married to her. Gemini can be very intriguing, but will only make for a happy marriage after middle age, when both partners are older and wiser. Younger Sagittarians often marry Aquarian women, but things quickly fall apart. Scorpios can make for an interesting relationship, but if the Sagittarius fails to comply, divorce is inevitable.

CAPRICORN

Practical, reserved Capricorn is one of the least sexual signs of the Zodiac. He views sex as an idle way to pass the time, and something he can live without, until he wants to start a family. He tends to marry late, and almost never divorces. Young Capricorns are prone to suppressing their sexual desires, and only discover them later in life, when they have already achieved everything a real man needs – a career and money. We'll be frank – Capricorn is not the best lover, but he can compensate by being caring, attentive, and showering you with valuable gifts. Ever cautious, Capricorn loves to schedule his sexual relationships, and this is something partners will just have to accept. Women should understand that Capricorn needs some help relaxing – perhaps with alcohol. They prefer inconspicuous, unassuming women, and run away from a fashion plate.

The best partners for a Capricorn are Virgo, Taurus, or Scorpio. Cancers might catch his attention, and if they marry, it is likely to be for life. Capricorn is able to easily dominate Pisces, and Pisces-Capricorn is a well-known "slave and master" combination. Relationships with Leos tend to be erratic, and they are unlikely to wed. Aries might make for a cozy family at first, but things will cool off quickly, and often, the marriage only lasts as long as Capricorn is unwilling to make a change in his life.

AQUARIUS

Aquarian men are mercurial, and often come off as peculiar, unusual, or aloof, and detached. Aquarians are turned on by anything novel or strange, and they are constantly looking for new and interesting people. They are stimulated by having a variety of sexual partners, but they consider this to simply be normal life, rather than sexually immoral. Aquarians are unique – they are more abstract than realistic, and can be cold and incomprehensible, even in close relationships. Once an Aquarius gets married, he will try to remain within the realm of decency, but often fails. An Aquarian's partners need uncommon patience, as nothing they do can restrain him. Occasionally, one might encounter another kind of Aquarius – a responsible, hard worker, and exemplary family man.

The best matches for an Aquarius are female fellow Aquarians, Libras, and Sagittarians. When Aquarius seeks out yet another affair, he is not choosy, and will be happy with anyone.

PISCES

Pisces is the most eccentric sign of the Zodiac. This is reflected in his romantic tendencies and sex life. Pisces men become very dependent on those with whom they have a close relationship. Paradoxically, they are simultaneously crafty and childlike when it comes to playing games, and they are easily deceived. As a double bodied sign, Pisces rarely marry just once, as they are very sexual, easily fall in love, and are constantly seeking their ideal. Pisces are very warm people, who love to take care of others and are inclined toward "slave-master" relationships, in which they are the submissive partner. But after catering to so many lovers, Pisces will remain elusive. They are impossible to figure out ahead of time – today, they might be declaring their love for you, but tomorrow, they may disappear – possibly forever! To a Pisces, love is a fantasy, illusion, and dream, and they might spend their whole lives in pursuit of it. Pisces who are unhappy in love are vulnerable to alcoholism or drug addiction.

Cancer and Scorpio make the best partners for a Pisces. He is also easily dominated by Capricorn and Libra, but in turn will conquer even a queen-like Leo. Often, they are fascinated by Geminis – if they marry, it will last a long time, but likely not forever. Relationships with Aries and Sagittarians are erratic, though initially, things can seem almost perfect.

Women

ARIES

Aries women are leaders. They are decisive, bold, and very protective. An Aries can take initiative and is not afraid to make the first move. Her ideal man is strong, and someone she can admire. But remember, at the slightest whiff of weakness, she will knock him off his pedestal. She does not like dull, whiny men, and thinks that there is always a way out of any situation. If she loves someone, she will be faithful. Aries women are too honest to try leading a double life. They are possessive, jealous, and not only will they not forgive those who are unfaithful, their revenge may be brutal; they know no limits. If you can handle an Aries, don't try to put her in a cage; it is best to give her a long leash. Periodically give her some space – then she will seek you out herself. She is sexual, and believe that anything goes in bed.

Her best partners are a Sagittarius or Leo. A Libra can make a good match after middle age, once both partners have grown wiser and settled down a bit. Gemini and Aquarius are only good partners during the initial phase, when everything is still new, but soon enough, they will lose interest in each other. Scorpios are good matches in bed, but only suitable as lovers.

TAURUS

Taurean women possess qualities that men often dream about, but rarely find in the flesh – they are soft, charming, practical, and reliable – they are very caring and will support their partner in every way. A Taurus is highly sexual, affectionate, and can show a man how to take pleasure to new heights. She is also strong and intense. If she is in love, she will be faithful. But when love fades away, she might find someone else on the side, though she will still fight to save her marriage, particularly if her husband earns good money. A Taurus will not tolerate a man who is disheveled or disorganized, and anyone dating her needs to always be on his toes. She will expect gifts, and likes being taken to expensive restaurants, concerts, and other events. If you argue, try to make the first peace offering, because a Taurus finds it very hard to do so – she might withdraw and ruminate for a long time. Never air your dirty laundry; solve all your problems one-on-one.

Scorpio, Virgo, Capricorn, and Cancer make the best matches. A relationship with an Aries or Sagittarius would be difficult. There is little attraction between a Taurus and a Leo, and initially Libras can make for a good partner in bed, but things will quickly cool off and fall apart. A Taurus and Aquarius make an interesting match – despite the difference in signs, their relationships are often lasting, and almost lifelong.

GEMINI

Gemini women are social butterflies, outgoing, and they easily make friends, and then break off the friendship, if people do not hold their interest. A Gemini falls in love hard, is very creative, and often fantasizes about the object of her affection. She is uninterested in sex without any attachment, loves to flirt, and, for the most part, is not particularly affectionate. She dreams of a partner who is her friend, lover, and a romantic, all at once. A Gemini has no use for a man who brings nothing to the table intellectually. That is a tall order, so Geminis often divorce and marry several times. Others simply marry later in life. Once you have begun a life together, do not try to keep her inside – she needs to travel, explore, socialize, attend events and go to the theater. She cannot tolerate possessive men, so avoid giving her the third degree, and remember that despite her flirtatious and social nature, she is, in fact, faithful – as long as you keep her interested and she is in love. Astrologists believe that Geminis do not know what they need until age 29 or 30, so it is best to hold off on marriage until then.

Leo and Libra make the best matches. A relationship with a Cancer is likely, though complex, and depends solely on the Cancer's affection. A Gemini and Sagittarius can have an interesting, dynamic relationship, but these are two restless signs, which might only manage to get together after ages 40-45, once they have had enough thrills out of life and learned to be patient. Relationships with a Capricorn are very difficult, and almost never happen. The honeymoon stage can be wonderful with a Scorpio, but each partner will eventually go their own way, before ending things. A Gemini and Pisces union can also be very interesting – they are drawn to each other, and can have a wonderful relationship, but after a while, the cracks start to show and things will fall apart. An Aquarius is also not a bad match, but they will have little sexual chemistry.

CANCER

Cancers can be divided into two opposing groups. The first includes a sweet and gentle creature who is willing to dedicate her life to her husband and children. She is endlessly devoted to her husband, especially if he makes a decent living and remains faithful. She views all men as potential husbands, which means it is dangerous to strike up a relationship with her if your intentions are not serious; she can be anxious and clingy, sensitive and prone to crying. It is better to break things to her gently, rather than directly spitting out the cold, hard truth. She wants a man who can be a provider, though she often earns well herself. She puts money away for a rainy day, and knows how to be thrifty, for the sake of others around her, rather than only for herself. She is an excellent cook and capable of building an inviting home for her loved ones. She is enthusiastic in bed, a wonderful wife, and a caring mother.

The second type of Cancer is neurotic, and capable of creating a living hell for those around her. She believes that the world is her enemy, and manages to constantly find new intrigue and machinations.

Another Cancer, Virgo, Taurus, Scorpio, and Pisces make the best matches. A Cancer can often fall in love with a Gemini, but eventually, things will grow complicated, as she will be exhausted by a Gemini's constant mood swings and cheating. A Cancer and Sagittarius will initially have passionate sex, but things will quickly cool off. A relationship with a Capricorn is a real possibility, but only later in life, as while they are young, they are likely to fight and argue constantly. Cancer can also have a relationship with an Aries, but this will not be easy.

LEO

Leos are usually beautiful or charming, and outwardly sexual. And yet, appearances can be deceiving – they are not actually that interested in sex. Leo women want to be the center of attention and men running after them boosts their self-esteem, but they are more interested in their career, creating something new, and success than sex. They often have high-powered careers and are proud of their own achievements. Their partners need to be strong; if a Leo feels a man is weak, she can carry him herself for a while- before leaving him. It is difficult for her to find a partner for life, as chivalrous knights are a dying breed, and she is not willing to compromise. If you are interested in a Leo, take the initiative, admire her, and remember that even a queen is still a woman. Timid men or tightwads need not apply. Leos like to help others, but they don't need a walking disaster in their life. If they are married and in love, they are usually faithful, and petty gossip isn't their thing. Leo women make excellent mothers, and are ready to give their lives to their children. Their negative traits include vanity and a willingness to lie, in order to make themselves look better.

Sagittarius, Aries, and Libra make the best matches. Leos can also have an interesting relationship with a Virgo, though both partners will weaken each other. Life with a Taurus will lead to endless arguments – both signs are very stubborn, and unwilling to give in. Leos and Pisces are another difficult pair, as she will have to learn to be submissive if she wants to keep him around. A relationship with a Capricorn will work if there is a common denominator, but they will have little sexual chemistry. Life with a Scorpio will be turbulent to say the least, and they will usually break up later in life.

VIRGO

Virgo women are practical, clever, and often duplicitous. Marrying one isn't for everyone. She is a neat freak to the point of annoying those around her. She is also an excellent cook, and strives to ensure her children receive the very best by teaching them everything, and preparing them for a bright future. She is also thrifty – she won't throw money around, and, in fact, won't even give it to her husband. She has no time for rude, macho strongmen, and is suspicious of spendthrifts. She will not be offended if you take her to a cozy and modest café rather than an elegant restaurant. Virgos are masters of intrigue, and manage to outperform every other sign of the Zodiac in this regard. Virgos love to criticize everyone and everything; to listen to them, the entire world is simply a disaster and wrong, and only she is the exception to this rule. Virgos are not believed to be particularly sexual, but there are different variations when it comes to this. Rarely, one finds an open-minded Virgo willing to try anything, and who does it all on a grand scale – but she is rather the exception to this general rule.

The best matches for a Virgo are Cancer, Taurus, and Capricorn. She also can get along well with a Scorpio, but will find conflict with Sagittarius. A Pisces will strike her interest, but they will rarely make it down the aisle. She is often attracted to an Aquarius, but they would drive each other up the wall were they to actually marry. An Aries forces Virgo to see another side of life, but here, she will have to learn to conform and adapt.

LIBRA

Female Libras tend to be beautiful, glamorous, or very charming. They are practical, tactical, rational, though they are adept at hiding these qualities behind their romantic and elegant appearance. Libras are drawn to marriage, and are good at imagining the kind of partner they need. They seek out strong, well-off men and are often more interested in someone's social status and bank account than feelings. The object of their affection needs to be dashing, and have a good reputation in society. Libras love expensive things, jewelry, and finery. If they are feeling down, a beautiful gift will instantly cheer them up. They will not tolerate scandal or conflict, and will spend all their energy trying to keep the peace, or at least the appearance thereof. They do not like to air their dirty laundry, and will only divorce in extreme circumstances. They are always convinced they are right and react to any objections as though they have been insulted. Most Libras are not particularly sexual, except those with Venus or the Moon in Scorpio.

Leos, Geminis, and Aquarians make good matches. Libra women are highly attracted to Aries men - this is a real case of opposites attract. They can get along with a Sagittarius, though he will find that Libras are too proper and calm. Capricorn, Pisces, and Cancer are all difficult matches. Things will begin tumultuously with a Taurus, before each partner goes his or her own way.

SCORPIO

Scorpio women may appear outwardly restrained, but there is much more bubbling below the surface. They are ambitious with high self-esteem, but often wear a mask of unpretentiousness. They are the true power behind the scenes, the one who holds the family together, but never talk about it. Scorpios are strong-willed, resilient, and natural survivors. Often, Scorpios are brutally honest, and expect the same out of those around them. They do not like having to conform, and attempt to get others to adapt to them, as they honestly believe everyone will be better off that way. They are incredibly intuitive, and not easily deceived. They have an excellent memory, and can quickly figure out which of your buttons to push. They are passionate in bed, and their temperament will not diminish with age. When she is sexually frustrated, a Scorpio will throw all of her energy into her career or her loved ones. She is proud, categorical, and "if you don't do it right, don't do it at all" is her motto. Scorpio cannot be fooled, and she will not forgive any cheating. Will she cheat herself? Yes! But it will not break up her family, and she will attempt to keep it a secret. Scorpios are usually attractive to men, even if they are not particularly beautiful. They keep a low profile, though they always figure out their partner, and give them some invisible sign. There is also another, selfish type of Scorpio, who will use others for as long as they need them, before unceremoniously casting them aside.

Taurus is a good match; they will have excellent sexual chemistry and understand each other. Scorpio and Gemini are drawn to each other, but are unlikely to stay together long enough to actually get married. Cancer can be a good partner as well, but Cancers are possessive, while Scorpios do not like others meddling in their affairs, though they can later resolve their arguments in bed. Scorpio and Leo are often found together, but their relationship can also be very complicated. Leos are animated and chipper, while Scorpios, who are much deeper and more stubborn, see Leos as not particularly serious or reliable. One good example of this is Bill (a Leo) and Hillary (a Scorpio) Clinton. Virgo can also make a good partner, but when Scorpio seemingly lacks emotions, he will look for them elsewhere. Relationships with Lira are strange and very rare. Scorpio sees Libra as too insecure, and Libra does not appreciate Scorpio's rigidity. Two Scorpios together make an excellent marriage! Sagittarius and Scorpio are unlikely to get together, as she will think he is shallow and rude. If they do manage to get married, Scorpio's drive and persistence is the only thing that will make the marriage last. Capricorn is also not a bad match, and while Scorpio finds Aquarius attractive, they will rarely get married, as they are simply speaking different languages! Things are alright with a Pisces, as both signs are emotional, and Pisces can let Scorpio take the lead when necessary.

SAGITTARIUS

Sagittarius women are usually charming, bubbly, energetic, and have the gift of gab. They are kind, sincere, and love people. They are also straightforward, fair, and very ambitious, occasionally to the point of irritating those around them. But telling them something is easier than not telling them, and they often manage to win over their enemies. Sagittarius tends to have excellent intuition, and she loves to both learn and teach others. She is a natural leader, and loves taking charge at work and at home. Many Sagittarian women have itchy feet, and prefer all kinds of travel to sitting at home. They are not particularly good housewives – to be frank, cooking and cleaning is simply not for them. Their loved ones must learn to adapt to them, but Sagittarians themselves hate any pressure. They are not easy for men to handle, as Sagittarians want to be in charge. Sagittarius falls in love easily, is very sexual and temperamental, and may marry multiple times. Despite outward appearances, Sagittarius is a very lonely sign. Even after she is married with children, she may continue living as if she were alone; you might say she marches to the beat of her own drum. Younger

PISCES

Pisces women are very adaptable, musically inclined, and erotic. They possess an innate earthly wisdom, and a good business sense. Pisces often reinvent themselves; they can be emotional, soft, and obstinate, as well as sentimental, at times. Their behavioral changes can be explained by frequent ups and downs. Pisces is charming, caring, and her outward malleability is very attractive to men. She is capable of loving selflessly, as long as the man has something to love. Even if he doesn't, she will try and take care of him until the very end. Pisces' greatest fear is poverty. They are intuitive, vulnerable, and always try to avoid conflict. They love to embellish the truth, and sometimes alcohol helps with this. Rarely, one finds extremely unbalanced, neurotic and dishonest Pisces, who are capable of turning their loved ones' lives into a living Hell!

Taurus, Capricorn, Cancer, and Scorpio make the best matches. She will be greatly attracted to a Virgo, but a lasting relationship is only likely if both partners are highly spiritual. Any union with a Libra is likely to be difficult and full of conflict. Pisces finds Gemini attractive, and they may have a very lively relationship – for a while. Occasionally, Pisces ends up with a Sagittarius, but she will have to fade into the background and entirely submit to him. If she ends up with an Aquarius, expect strong emotional outbursts, and a marriage that revolves around the need to raise their children.

Tatiana Borsch

Printed in Great Britain
by Amazon